Go for No!®

for

Network Marketing

D0166532

Richard Fenton, Andrea Waltz,

and

RAY HIGDON

Copyright © March 2017

Courage Crafters, Inc.

ISBN 978-0-9774393-7-9

DISCLAIMER:

What would you think if we told you there was a success strategy so powerful it could deliver immediate results? So simple it could be learned in less than a day? And so reproducible that anyone could master it?

Well, there is just such a strategy, and in the pages to come you're going to learn exactly what it is—and how to apply it.

Everyone loves the sound of the word *yes*.

It's so positive.

So empowering.

And then there's

NO.

For most people, no is just the opposite.

Negative.

Draining.

The antithesis of yes.

But what if everyone's wrong?

What if NO was actually the most empowering word in the world?

What Others Are Saying About
Go for No!®

"There are three things I really like about this book; it's easy to read, it's fun to read, and it totally changed the way I think about failure."

— Roland Bonay

"This book changed my life as a salesperson. The lessons in this book are incredible. This is a quick, entertaining read. This should be mandatory for anyone who works in sales. Stop getting in your own way. Learn how failure is a GOOD and positive thing. I have recommended this book to everyone. Absolutely worth the read. Motivational and inspiring."

— Katy Corbeil

"This book is truly a life changer! I highly recommend this book!!"

— Clarissa Winchester

"If the world was my way, every person would read this book... makes you truly FEEL the possibilities in every avenue of your life. You will not feel the same about your own potential after reading this, and the world will seem a bit brighter, no matter how positive a perspective you have."

— Christina M. Pegram

"We all know no single book can change a life. Go for No!® can inspire you to greatness. The world of network marketing is opportunity driven and this book is a home run for the novice or the pro."

— Dan McCormick

"Go for No!® teaches you a new way of looking at the process of prospecting and goal setting... one of the first books I was recommended to read by my incredibly supportive up-line. I highly recommend it, too."

— Aaron Masterson

"Go for No!® by Fenton and Waltz is storytelling at its finest! The book has my recommendation because not only is it an easy and enjoyable read, but the message is quite clear. It is a paradigm shift in traditional thinking about sales and the examples are simple to follow."

— Val Heisey

"How do you handle being told no? This book touches on that. I love it, and you will need this as well when you work in the field of networking! Read this book if you've been getting a lot of NOes."

— Stacy Printerson

"Quick read but the value is beyond measure for those having trouble managing rejection in sales. Go for No!® has changed the way I look at my network marketing, direct sales business. Great story. Got the message out succinctly. The concepts are easy to understand. Bravo!"

— Heather Koenigon

"Failing your way to success may seem crazy, but it surely works! If you're looking for just the thing to jumpstart your career in sales or network marketing, THIS is absolutely the best book to start with! Very quick read with content that is both entertaining and valuable."

— Tracy Moore

"If you are a sales professional, a small-business owner, or if you are in the industry of network marketing (or direct selling) you can't afford to ignore this book. The principles outlined may have a tremendously powerful impact on your ability to grow your business like you never imagined."

— Kumar Gauraw

"Looking for something inspirational and practical yet easy to read? Go for No!® immediately reminds me of the poem "The Road Not Taken" by Robert Frost. Each chapter is only a few pages long; the concepts are easy to understand, but you still need to put in the work."

— Matthew Timothy

"This book will help you cultivate the right mindset to help you on your way to achieving your dreams and ambitions. The story touched me deeply and the message will live on inside of me for the rest of my life."

— Alan Abrahams

"The beauty of this book is that the lessons are simple and easy to understand. Like all-powerful lessons, the implementation is where the value lies. It will cause you to rethink a number of your commonly held beliefs."

— John Chancellor

A Message from the Authors of
Go for No!®

Hello, Richard Fenton and Andrea Waltz here. It's nice to meet you, if only through these pages.

The truth is not many people use our actual names when referring to us. Family and friends, of course. Clients we do business with. But to the majority of people we're simply known as *The Go for No!®* people.

Good branding, huh?

That's okay. We designed it that way—because remembering our names is nowhere near as important as remembering the concept.

Because *Go for No!®* isn't just a book title. Or a catchphrase. Or a trademark. It's a million-dollar idea. A multi-million-dollar idea. And it can be a multi-million-dollar idea for you, too.

For nearly a decade we've helped thousands of salespeople, managers, entrepreneurs, and network-marketing professionals achieve breakthrough levels of performance by helping them overcome self-imposed limitations and fears of failure and rejection.

Our personal story is a *Go for No!®* story in and of itself.

We met where we worked—in the training department at LensCrafters, the eyewear retailer. We had important-sounding titles, above-average salaries, and company cars. We had pension plans, 401k retirement packages, and health insurance. For all intents and purposes, we had what everyone wants. Great jobs with a growing company and job security.

And then we quit.

The reason we left our safe, secure corporate jobs was so we could become entrepreneurs and launch our own training company. To be honest, we were scared to death, but we did it anyway.

We cobbled together a few training program descriptions, bought a fax machine (back in those days you weren't a real business without a fax machine), and began calling companies to see if they would be interested in hiring us.

We mailed brochures and dialed the phone for five straight months, and for five months all we heard was: "No."

On the 153rd day of calling, we got our first yes. And it was a big one. Immediately after that, we got our second yes—and it was even bigger. We were on our way.

Since then we have worked with some of the most successful organizations in the world, including Samsonite, American Express, JCPenney, Tommy Hilfiger, REI, RE/MAX, PetSmart—and within the world of network marketing/direct selling, Pampered Chef, Utility Warehouse, Juice Plus, Ambit Energy, Forever Living, Arbonne, and many others.

But the thing we're proudest of is our #1 Amazon best-selling book, *Go for No!®*.

Originally published in 2000, *Go for No!®* was our second book. The first was a sixty-four-page fable called *Retail Magic*, which was written as a promotional piece to establish ourselves when we first launched our company. To our surprise, *Retail Magic* sold in excess of forty thousand copies— and this was before Amazon. The books were sold exclusively by phone and fax machine orders (the fax machine came in handy after all.)

So we had high hopes when *Go for No!®* was published, and we sent five hundred review copies to various magazines and business leaders. The initial sales were disappointing. This is not to say we didn't sell any we did. Just not in the numbers we'd hoped.

In any case, the book helped us refine our message and our training and get more clients. But then, as things tend to happen, we got lucky.

We were attending a convention in Las Vegas and had brought twenty copies of the book with us to give away. On the last day, we still had one book left.

"Give it to that guy," Andrea said, pointing to a man sitting in the row in front of me. "He mentioned he was in sales." We gave the man the book, and with that we were off to the airport for our flight home.

Three days later, the phone rang. "My name is Tom Schaff," he said. "I just finished reading your book, and I have to tell you it's one of the best business books I've ever read."

"Thanks," I said.

"But there's something else I need to tell you," Tom said. "Are you open to feedback?"

"Sure. What is it?"

"It's the cover," Tom said. "You guys have written one of the best books ever, with one of the worst covers in the history of publishing. In fact, I threw it away when I got home from Vegas, and then fished it out of the garbage can this morning just for the heck of it. Now, if you're willing to hire a cover designer and have the cover replaced, I'll take five thousand copies."

We had the cover redesigned, sold Tom five thousand copies, and the rest is history. Today, *Go for No!*® has sold somewhere in excess of four hundred thousand copies and is still on the Amazon top twenty sales best-seller list over a decade later.

Now we've partnered with good friend and network marketing expert Ray Higdon to help us create the ultimate companion guide to *Go for No!*®, specifically for this special profession—which is what you are now holding in your hands (or reading on Kindle perhaps.)

To be honest, we should have done it sooner.

In any case, here it is. We hope you love it!

Richard Fenton & Andrea Waltz
February 2017

A Note from Co-Author
RAY HIGDON

July 15, 2009, was the day I decided to get serious about network marketing. It was the day I read Go for No!® *for the first time.*

I was sick and tired of being in the state of victimhood.

I was sick and tired of being in a non-producing state.

I don't know if my self-esteem was as high as when I was just starting out as an entrepreneur, but my determination was there and I greatly valued where I wanted to go more than my self-image.

Then I developed a new vision.

I had a renewed sense of drive.

I went on a mission to collect twenty noes per day— everyday, without fail—and the level of success I attained was extraordinary by any measure.

With the help of the concepts in the book—combined with the inner vision of who I wanted to become—I taught myself to become immune to rejection and criticism from others.

After that, my success exploded.

This is why I am so pleased to have been asked by Richard and Andrea to co-author this Go for No!® *companion guide, specifically designed for the network marketing community.*

All the best...

Ray Higdon

N.O.

Two Small Letters.
Big Difference.

We all suffer from fear of failure, rejection, and hearing the word *no* to some degree.

We all have some self-imposed limitations that prevent us from achieving our full potential.

No one is totally immune.

Don't worry.

It doesn't have to stay that way.

What if no could actually be the most empowering word in the world? What if you could achieve every quota, hit every income goal, and reach every personal dream by simply hearing no more often?

And what if you discovered that right now—this very minute— you were only two letters away from greatness? Two letters away from breakthrough performance. Two letters from everything you ever wanted.

As kids we weren't fazed at all when we heard the word *no*. We shrugged it off, laughed at it, flicked it away like a bug. But somewhere along the way this natural sense of tenacity was lost. Or, worse still, it was drummed out of us.

But what if, starting today, you could get that tenacity back?

What if, starting today, the word *no* stopped stopping you?

What if, starting today, the word *no* actually started empowering you?

And what if, starting today, every time you heard the word *no* you became stronger? More powerful? More resilient?

And what if—in fact—having people tell you *no* actually became... *fun.*

What might happen then?

A Counter-Intuitive Concept

You are about to be introduced to a number of concepts, many of which may be counter-intuitive, forcing you to think in radically different ways.

Which reminds us of the story about the Zen master and student in search of knowledge. The Zen master is pouring tea as the student goes on and on about everything he has already learned. While the student is talking, he notices the Zen master has not only filled the cup, but he also continues pouring until the tea is spilling onto the table. The student says, "Zen master, can't you see the cup is overflowing?"

The Zen master replies, "You are like the cup, full to the top with what you already know. To learn something new, one must first be willing to empty their cup."

Can You Empty Your Cup?

To accept what we're about to tell you, it will be necessary for you to remove some of your current assumptions and beliefs about failure and success. And while you might not agree with some of what we have to share, we can assure you that these concepts are proven, and, as such, we ask that you keep an open mind. Sound fair?

Good.

Because we're about to share the key, central premise upon which this program is built—a premise that requires an open mind to accept it.

Ready? Okay, here goes.

The most guaranteed way to achieve success is...

To intentionally increase your failure rate.

In other words, the best way to hear yes more often and achieve your goals and dreams is to...

Go for No!®

The truth is, most people spend their lives doing everything within their power to seek success while simultaneously doing everything within their power to avoid failure—a recipe that virtually ensures average performance!

Increasing your failure rate is __the__ ultimate strategy for long-term, outstanding performance.

Because when you increase your failure, success will show up at your door in greater quantities than you ever could have imagined.

So, What About You?

When you hear the word *no*, what does that mean to you? How do you respond—both internally in your mind and externally in your actions? This is important because it is this—and quite often this alone—that ultimately spells the difference between achieving long-term success and eventual failure for millions of people all over the planet.

It's not age or gender...

It's not training or skill...

It's not the product or service being offered...

And it's not the economy either.

It's the relationship you have with NO—what you think and feel when you hear it. How you internalize and respond to hearing no—whether you seek opportunities to hear more noes or run from them—is the single most important factor in determining the level of success you will achieve in your business and your life.

In fact, we're willing to go out on a ledge here and say that if you are not currently achieving the level of success you want in your life, you are probably not failing often enough.

But it's not just you. Most people do not fail anywhere nearly enough. In fact, most people spend the majority of their waking hours doing the exact opposite. They spend enormous mental and physical effort trying to avoid failure with everything they have—a strategy guaranteed to produce average results and a mediocre income.

The Greatest Success Strategy in the World

One of the great ironies of life is the fact that winners fail more often than losers because they understand that intentionally and dramatically increasing your failure rate *is* the greatest success strategy in the world.

Now, from our experience, there are a certain percentage of people who will read these words and think: *Huh, increase your failure? That's an interesting theory.*

Let us assure you, achieving success by going for no is not a theory:

It's a proven fact.

Achieving increased levels of success by intentionally increasing your failure rate works, and we've got the track record, testimonials, and results to prove it.

The *Go for No!®* concepts and strategies you are about to learn have been used, field-tested, and have already helped tens of thousands of individuals and organizations achieve unheard of levels of success.

But What About Network Marketing?

But what about network marketing? Does it work there, too? It's a question we knew you'd ask.

That's why we've included numerous *Go for No!®* stories throughout this book from people just like you who have used the concepts to grow—and explode—their businesses.

So, if you approach the ideas in this book as interesting stuff that might be worth a try, you'll be robbing yourself and your team of the results you both deserve.

We're asking you to have faith. We're asking you to believe. We're asking you to try the things we propose in this book before passing judgment.

If you do, the results will truly amaze you.

Everyone "Sells"

Now, as you work your way through this book you'll notice that we use the terms *sales* and *salesperson* often and repeatedly. Everyone sells!

In our own way, each and every one of us is a salesperson. Yes, the person attempting to sell a prospect a house, car, boat, sweater, or insurance policy is clearly selling. But so is:

- The entrepreneur raising money to start a business...
- The Girl Scout selling cookies in early spring...

- The author trying to get their book published...
- The actor auditioning for a role...
- The high school senior asking a girl to the prom...
- The network-marketing professional inviting a friend, neighbor, relative, or stranger to look at their opportunity...
- The mom or dad trying desperately to get their two-year old to eat their peas.

Each is engaged in the selling process, whether they define it as sales or not. Each must overcome failure and rejection to be successful. Each must find the courage and tenacity to put themselves, their product, and their services out there—sometimes over and over again—to persist until successful.

A Life Philosophy

Finally, *Go for No!*® isn't just a sales philosophy—it's a life philosophy.

We like to say you can achieve virtually everything you want if you're just willing to hear no often enough. And it's true. So often we lose out on the things we want to have, do, and be in life simply because we fear asking and being rejected.

So whether it's asking a guy or girl out on a date, asking for a raise, asking for a better table in a restaurant, or for an upgrade to a better view at a hotel for your anniversary night – all of these everyday life choices require one choice to be made first: do I have the courage to get a no?

This book can help you say yes.

Jackie Christiansen

I remember being a network marketing newbie - with stars in my eyes, big dreams of immediate success, travel, and a business that would grow each day, each month, each year. It started off great; the first two weeks in the business and I had recruited just about everyone I had spoken to - I had enrolled 11 people in two weeks and it felt amazing! I thought wow, this is so easy! Why didn't I do this before? No one can say no to me! Who can I talk to next?

At the time, I wouldn't dare go to my family and friends so I talked to everyone that I met - at the grocery store, at the gym, standing in line at the cleaners, the local Kinko's store, you name it! One of the first calls I made was to a fellow personal trainer and retired professional football player and he even said yes! It felt great when a few friends called me, asking what I was doing and said they wanted to do it too. I immediately fell in love with this business and I was on fire and hooked because I was going to be a millionaire in this industry!

Fast forward six weeks later...

Out of the 11 people I had enrolled, 9 had quit. They all had their reasons and all were legitimate. Sometimes life just gets in the way of one's plans. One of these people was a woman whose husband had opened a tattoo parlour and he needed her full-time help. One of the friends that joined me had zero support from his wife and she told him to quit. Believe me when I tell you that each one of the others that quit all had good reasons too. Sometimes it's just the wrong timing.

I had looked at my organizational structure in the back office and I was devastated. My organization that was thriving and full of hope and promise was suddenly dead.

I remember standing in my kitchen that night and feeling defeated, hopeless and thinking maybe I had made a big mistake. I couldn't believe it. I thought, how could this be?

Then the thought occurred to me that I could quit. I could give up. I could walk away and pretend it never happened. Maybe that would take away the pain and failure I was feeling.

Something else happened at that moment. I realized I had an important decision to make. I had two choices. I could quit and never know what my future could have been. What if one of the people I sponsored did incredibly well and was super successful, made a ton of money and built a huge organization? I realized that I would be missing out and I would have regret for the rest of my life. I couldn't stand what that would feel like. I had been able to put myself in that position in the future, where I forecasted what it would be like to feel that sense of loss and it was very painful.

Something else had happened during that moment too - I remembered my upline's advice. She would speak on the weekly calls and say the same thing over and over. She said that whatever you do in this business, you don't ever want to quit. To use her exact words, she said "Don't ever, ever, ever quit this business." I had listened to those calls every week, and her advice had stuck. She was right.

There was one other piece of advice and perspective that helped as well. It was my husband's encouraging, and simple advice which didn't sound so great at the time, and in fact, I still remember how I hated his idea. He said "Jackie, that's okay, you can just start over." And that is exactly what I did.

This is one of the most important decisions I have ever made. It's a decision that not only impacted me, but my family as well. You see, I went on to replace my full-time income within 7 months, close my personal training business and do this business full-time. Within 20 months, I had also replaced my husband's full-time income as an aerospace engineer and retired him at age 49. Dana has since joined me in the network marketing industry and is my business partner.

This industry has changed our life forever. It has increased the quality of our lives, our family life, and given us things I always dreamed of. I know I can help other people achieve their dreams as well.

I want to leave you with some important advice. Know that you have the power to decide how your life is going to go. You have the power to succeed and no one can stop you. The power of the human spirit is so strong it cannot be defeated if your dream and goals are important enough to you.

Allow your mind to control your emotions, not the other way around. Learn to use your mind to help you achieve the things that are important to you in this life. You hold the power to your future. Here's to you and your incredible network marketing success!

- Jackie Christiansen, Network Marketing
Industry Leader & #1 Top Female Income Earner.
www.JackieChristiansen.com

Go for No!® and The Law of Attraction

Before we move on, there is one more small perceptual challenge we run into a lot, so we thought we'd get it out of the way right now.

It is about the law of attraction.

First, it's important for you to know that we are strong believers in the law of attraction. We love *The Secret*. We've watched the movie many times. We're friends with some of the people who appeared in it.

So if we believe in the law of attraction, how can we tell people to '*Go for No!*'? Do we really want people to be attracting more failure into their lives? Isn't that negative thinking? No, it's not. Here's why:

We are 100 percent positive that YES and NO are a package deal. You simply can't have one without the other—not in major quantities at least.

So if what you really want is to hear YES more often, then you want to hear NO more often, too.

By attracting more NOes into your life, you automatically attract more YESES into your life.

If A = B and B = C, then A = C.

YES is the destination → NO is how you get there.

That's the extent of our math skills, so please don't ask for a deeper explanation. But trust us when we tell you, the proof is in the doing.

(Note: If for any reason you still think NO is negative, keep reading. It's a sign you may need this book more than you realize.)

Definitions of Failure and Success

Failure is, without a doubt, one of the most emotionally loaded words in the English language. And it's traditionally one of the experiences we naturally try to avoid.

In fact, for many people, the very idea of failing is enough to stop them dead in their tracks.

Success, on the other hand, is an often mythical, nearly magical concept for the majority of people—a lifetime pursuit. Who doesn't want to be seen as a success?

This is why so many people will do virtually anything—and sacrifice so much—to achieve it.

Anything but be labeled a failure, that is.

And therein lies the rub!

To achieve meaningful success—to be considered successful by virtually any standard—you must be willing to fail.

There are <u>no</u> <u>exceptions</u> to this rule.

And the more significant the success, the more significant the risk of failure will be, both in terms of quantity of failures experienced and the magnitude of those failures.

So how do we reconcile this predicament?

The answers lay in our personal, internal definitions of failure and success.

Success and failure are concepts that can be defined in many ways. For our purposes here, let's define them as follows:

Success means hitting a target, reaching a goal, or achieving a defined objective. In other words, getting what you want.

Conversely, failure means falling short of a target or not reaching a goal or achieving a defined objective. In other words, *not* getting what you want.

But here's an idea that turns things around entirely:

What if the goal—what you're trying to achieve—is to intentionally increase in the number of times we get others to say no to us?

What if hearing no more often was the goal? Is it possible to actually be successful at intentionally achieving failure?

The answer is: *yes.*

Of course it is.

If hearing NO more often is the goal, then hearing NO more often becomes an achievement.

The problem is most people tend to think in absolutes. In the minds of people with rigid thinking, opposites must be just that—they must be opposites. Rigid thinking prevents many people from allowing failure and success—yes and no—to co-exist on the same end of the performance spectrum.

With the right reorganization of thought, yes and no don't have to be opposites.

Interestingly, the idea that yes and no (or failure and success) are opposites is very much a Western point of view. In the East, failure and success are intermingled, like two halves of a yin and yang symbol. One half is distinctly black and the other half is distinctly white—but they are intermingled.

Both are required to make the whole.

In this way, the Eastern perspective, including success and failure, is much more enlightened.

For example, consider this classic interchange between a Zen master and his student:

> Student: *Master, if one attempts to fail and succeeds, is he a failure or a success?*
>
> Zen Master: *Yes! Exactly!*

In the minds of many people, success is considered good—and failure is considered bad.

Opposites of one another.

But what if they're not? What if yes and no are *not* opposites, but simply opposite sides of the same coin? What if rather than being enemies, yes and no are partners? Companions? Even friends? Like the Lone Ranger and Tonto: one the hero, and the other the sidekick.

The problem in the movies is that the hero gets all the glory, while the sidekick gets stuck tending to the hero's horse.

To reach your full potential you must stop thinking of success and failure as opposites—and you must merge them into the yin and yang they really are. Opposite sides of the same coin that rely and depend on one another. In the same way that every coin has two sides, all achievement has two sides.

YES AND NO ARE JUST OPPOSITE SIDES OF THE SAME COIN.

Yes. *No.*

Success. *Failure.*

Heads. *Tails.*

Now, here's where it gets really interesting.

The more failure one experiences, the more success they will experience as well. To illustrate the point, let's use the example of flipping a coin.

In our example, let's say that every time the coin comes up heads, you've received a yes—and every time the coin comes up tails, you've received a no.

Now, imagine you are allowed to play the game one of two ways:

- You can flip the coin as many times as you want until tails comes up. When you get tails, the game is over. You have to stop playing.

- Alternatively, you can flip the coin as many times as you want—period. When you get tails, the game isn't over. You can keep playing.

Here's the question:

Which way have you been playing the game in your business? In your life?

Hear this now and hear it clearly:

You must abandon the notion that the best way to increase your success is to decrease your failure.

The best way to increase your success is to increase your failure!

But we do need to make one thing clear:

When we talk about failure we are always talking about an event—not a person, not a career, not a life. The act of failing is very different from being a failure. You can fail (a lot) *without ever being a failure.*

Our Definition of Failure

Our definition is:

Failure is an undeniable sign of progress toward a goal.

To our mind, the only way to *be* a failure is to quit. Period. Anyone who is actively pursuing a goal or dream is *never* a failure—*they are success in progress.* Failure is never a permanent condition unless *you* decide it's permanent.

You must:

Get beyond the *willingness* to tolerate hearing no and learn to embrace it.

At this point you may be thinking: *Okay, I get it. All I need to do to be successful is to tolerate failure and rejection and be willing to hear no more often. Right?*

Wrong.

We don't want you to learn to *tolerate* failure. We don't want you to *fight through* it to get to yes. We want you to like it. We want you to embrace it. We want you to learn to love hearing the word *no.*

Love rejection? Love hearing no?

For most people, simply *increasing* the number of times they hear no in a given day, week, month, or year is a mental stretch. Are we suggesting now that, in addition to increasing your failure rate, you should also learn to enjoy it?

Yes, we are.

Well, at least to a degree.

Here's a question for you: where is it written that rejection has to be awful?

What if hearing no could simply be annoying? Or maybe simply amusing?

Or—for that matter—what if hearing no could become exciting?

Energizing?

Empowering?

That's right. What if you decided to turn every no you received into something that empowered you rather than something that deflated you?

What if every no you heard made you stronger rather than weaker?

Now, to be completely honest, enjoying hearing the word *no* doesn't happen overnight. Like most people, chances are good you have years of negative conditioning to overcome. There's some mental reprogramming that needs to happen to get to the point where no can become a true positive in your life.

But it can happen.

If you work on it long enough, it *will* happen.

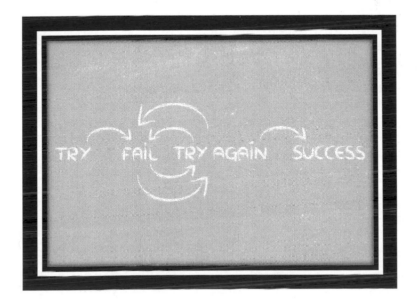

Ray Higdon's Take...

On Failure and Success

Here's my definition of failure: I set a goal I want to attain, but then I let something get in the way of attaining it. It reminds me of a great quote from George Zalucki:

> *"Commitment is doing the thing you said you would do, long after the mood you said it in has left you."*

For example, sometimes we want to accomplish something— and information is gathered that makes you realize you didn't really want it—that you no longer wish to pursue it. In this case, you are quitting because you decide it's intelligent for you to quit.

Over the years, I've gone back and forth on my definition of success, and the one that I've come to is that success is a combination of growth and contribution. I need to be in a constant state of growth to be successful.

I also need to be contributing, which can mean all kinds of different things. For me, contributing is helping others, working with my clients, helping them accomplish their goals, putting content out into the profession, speaking at different events, supporting others in their pursuit of their goals. I need to not just be growing as a person, but I also need to be growing as a company, too. I want every dollar we make to put more value into the marketplace. If it doesn't, we shouldn't create it. That means our company must be more profitable than the previous year if we're serious about growth.

To some people, contribution is writing a check to a charity. If that's your thing, good for you. But to me success requires both growth and contribution.

Tara Wilson

I got involved with network marketing in March of 2007. I had been to Mary Kay parties and jewelry parties, but I thought those people just worked for the company directly. I didn't know multi-level marketing even existed. My sister called me and said, "Look, I think there's something to this. It's a health product, and you like health, and at the end of the day you just have to find a few people that want to order it and you'll make some money."

Not knowing about the industry, of course you don't know that rejection is out there. The most harsh, awful, emotional rejection I had was from my best friend. And, when I say best friend: we were at each other's high school graduations, weddings, and she was in the room with my mother-in-law, my mother, and my sister when my first child was born.

Naturally I called her and I was very excited, because I had just gone to the meeting and I was feeling full of possibility. I told her everything and she was all excited - we were excited - we were going to do this and we were going to go big time!

The next day, I got an email from her. I'll never forget the way I felt when I got this email. I don't remember all of the words, but I remember this much: "Hey, I talked to my husband and he said it sounds like one of those pyramid things where you make money off your friends and family and we're just not willing to do that."

I was sitting in my office and all these thoughts were going through my head. I started welling up with tears: wow, she couldn't even pick up the phone and call me - my best friend?

And I sat there alone thinking; if my best friend, the person who trusts me, knows me, loves me probably more than anybody in the world outside my family doesn't see it, will I even have a chance? Will I really be able to do this? Who in the world would say "yes" then?

I went from really hurt, to angry. I remember thinking, I'm going to let this fuel me. Just because it's not her dream doesn't mean it's not going to be my dream, because I see it, and I know there's a lot of people out there, and a lot of people out there like me. Just because she doesn't see it doesn't mean that I can't succeed. I said, I don't know how, I don't know where, I don't know who, but I'll persist until I succeed just to prove her wrong, and honestly, that for many, many months was my motivation.

I'll never forget when we were talking about a year later. She asked me how it was going and I said, "Great! I'm making over $35,000 a month. I really wish you could have done this with me."

I retired myself a few months later, and I retired my husband five years in who owns his own business now. I'm a mom of three kids that gets to work from home. I've built teams now that have hundreds of thousands of people in 12 countries just because I didn't give up.

- Tara Wilson, Stay at Home Mom and Multi 7-Figure Earner

The Five Failure Levels

Level 5:
Failing Exponentially

Level 4:
Failing Bigger & Faster

Level 3:
WANTingness to Fail

Level 2:
The Willingness to Fail

Level 1:
The Ability to Fail

Level #1: <u>The Ability to Fail</u>

Everyone on planet earth has the ability to fail. It's where we all start! What keeps most people at level-one status is their intense desire to avoid any form of failure at all costs. As a result, 80 percent of all people never move past this basic level.

Level #2: <u>The Willingness to Fail</u>

Level-two people develop the willingness to fail, which means they come to accept failure as a natural by-product of the process of seeking success. Fewer than 20 percent of all people make it to level two for any sustained period of time.

The next level may be the most important of all:

Level #3: <u>The Wantingness to Fail</u>

Having the *wantingness* to fail goes beyond mere tolerance or acceptance of failure as a part of life. *Wantingness* means developing the desire to fail with the inner faith that personal and financial growth will follow. Fewer than 5 percent of all people ever get to level three.

Level #4: <u>Failing Bigger and Faster</u>

The people who ascend to level four are those who have come to the conclusion that if failing is good, then failing faster is better. And not just failing faster—if one is going to increase their failure rate, they should do it going after big goals that are worthy of the effort.

Finally, there's...

Level #5: <u>Failing Exponentially</u>

This final level is a function of management and team leadership for those rare individuals who understand that massive success requires multiplication of effort. Level-five people enlist others to fail with them and for them, knowing that if individual failure means individual success, then group failure equals group—or team—success.

Ray Higdon's Take...

Getting Beyond Willingness to "Wantingness"

I remember when I was in middle school, and I was selling this candy called Airheads. I found this little drugstore, and I could get them for ten cents. They were cheaper than anywhere else, and I would go sell them for a quarter. I was moving like ninety to a hundred a day. Just doing that made me a bit different from other kids in middle school since most kids aren't thinking about how to make money.

Even at that age there were kids who would say, "Oh, you're the kid that sells those stupid Airheads, right?" I think getting past deep concerns about looking good and avoiding criticism is the first step to being successful as an entrepreneur or a network marketer. If you can't get past the fear of criticism and learn to accept non-approval, then you have no shot at building a successful business or doing anything outside the ordinary. If you're not vaccinated from the existence of criticism, you'll never get to the point where you have the confidence to ask someone to buy something—let alone ask them to check out your company or watch a video.

When I decided I was going to leave corporate America, I was diving into books, studying how to be an entrepreneur, and discovering who I wanted to become. It was this vision that helped me become bulletproof.

I remember sitting in a Ruby Tuesday restaurant when I saw a group of very well-dressed guys sitting at a table right down the aisle from me. I got up and went over and said, "Hey guys, I do mortgages. I'd love to help you out." I look back and think how bold that was, but I was able to do it because my self-esteem was so high that I just didn't care.

Now, there have also been times when my self-esteem wasn't so high—like when the real-estate market crashed, and I lost everything. Here I was in foreclosure, dead broke, and being chased by bill collectors. My self-esteem was so low there was no way in heck I would have gone over to another table and introduced myself.

Kathleen Deggelman

I just celebrated my 10th year in Network Marketing! It has gone by so quickly. I have only been with two companies and while it has been a lot of work and certainly there have been lots of ups and downs, **every** aspect of my life is so much richer because of this profession and what we get to do, what we get to accomplish and who we get to become because of this choice! I could not imagine my life today if I had said no ten years ago. I feel incredibly blessed for the life I have lived and get to live.

So now that we have that out of the way, let me tell you about a few of the downs in those ups and downs.

I know what it feels like to have <u>every single family member</u> say no (and I have a very large family!) I know what it feels like to have family make fun of my choice, say no, try to talk me out of it and warn the rest of the family about what I was doing.

I know what it is like to push away from an email on the computer because I am about to cry at the words that were written to me about this choice by someone that I love very much.

I know what it is like to have my Mom trying to talk me out of this choice <u>two</u> years later when I was doing extremely well.

Fast forward a few years...

I still knew what it was like to have 95% of my family not be interested, involved or approve.

Fast forward a few more years:

I now finally have many of their approval and am called the entrepreneur of the family.

Would you like to know how I handled this massive rejection? I chose not to care. Of course, I still "cared" but I chose to let it fuel me. I chose to say quietly and under my breath, get out of my way and watch me.

I chose to become as successful as I could possibly be. Not to prove it to them but to prove it to myself. I didn't let anything stop me, not even the people I love the most. And eventually, it all worked out and I feel their love and support in terms of my business.

I learned to compartmentalize this area of my life in terms of their love and support. I knew they loved me and I knew they wanted the best for me and I knew they also didn't know what they were talking about. It wasn't my job to change their minds, or to lose sleep over it or even worse, to lose a relationship over my choice to become a network marketer.

I decided very early on that not one family meal or gathering would be "awkward" because they didn't see what I saw.

What if I had let them talk me out of it? What if I had let them sway my belief that I could be really good at this? I wouldn't have the health, relationships, adventures, wealth and loves of my life that I have today. I would have missed out on so much and thousands of people all around the world would not have been positively impacted either.

Sometimes—when it seems like nobody around you 'gets' what you are doing—that is when you have to go deep inside and make a decision that you are going to do this no matter what. I did that and I can tell you from the bottom of my heart, how grateful and happy I am that I did.

I wish you all the best and don't let anyone or anything stand in the way of what you believe and what you want and deserve in your life!

- Kathleen Deggelman, Top Network Marketing Professional, www.KathleenDeggelman.com

Your NQ (NO-Quotient™) is Significantly More Important Than Your IQ

As you already know, IQ stands for intelligence quotient. Interestingly, the vast majority of people do not know what their IQ is—but that's okay. Because knowing your IQ—or, for that matter, *having* a high IQ—is not all that critical when it comes to determining the level of success you will achieve in life.

In fact, when you look around, you see that the world is filled with lots of low-performing, high-IQ people—and lots of high-performing, low-IQ people.

The number that really matters in business and in life is your NQ—your *no quotient:*

- The number of times you are willing to hear no before succeeding...

- The amount of rejection you are willing to endure and keep going...

- The number of times you are willing to get k*nocked down and then get back up, knowing full well that you are almost certain to get knocked back down again...*

That is the number that determines greatness in today's world—perhaps the only number. Because the history of the world's greatest people, the movers and shakers and doers, is, in fact, a collection of stories of people with high NO-quotients.

When you look at the great success stories of our time, and you peel away the outer layer—the glitz and glamour of what is seen on the surface by the general public—what you discover are stories of what we might call "successful failures."

Virtually every successful person you can think of got there not just by failing, but usually through massive failure. Behind every story of success is a story of persistence, courage, tenacity, and a willingness to endure failure and rejection uncommon by any standard until successful.

Ray Higdon's Take...

IQ vs. Willingness to Fail

There are a lot of really, really smart people who are broke. Educated, pedigreed, degreed-up people who just don't make money. It's been fairly easy for me to locate people who are smarter than me, but I've also found that has absolutely nothing to do with making money. I don't want to say it's a hindrance. I won't go that far because I do have mentors who have helped me along the way and are really smart and intelligent. But I have seen a lot of people for whom intelligence has been a hindrance to their success. Their intelligence has hurt them because they're very aware of what things can go wrong. Sometimes that prevents them from taking action.

Years ago, a business partner and I started buying low-income rental homes. We were ignorance on fire! When we started, we had no idea we'd end up dealing with drug dealers, or that we would have people who would try to sue us. We didn't know all these things, and thank God we didn't know. Because if we had, we might not have moved as quickly as we did.

I can just tell you that intelligence, like high IQ, is absolutely not a requirement for any kind of success. That doesn't mean you shouldn't pursue getting smarter. I look for ways to educate myself all the time to get smarter and get better. I look around and see people who feel they're not smart enough to achieve success. But they're wrong.

I've met some incredibly successful people, especially in network marketing, that by all educational standards probably don't have a high IQ. People who would not be considered overly intelligent. But they're willing to play life a little differently than other people—to get their jersey dirty. To get criticized and rejected over and over and over. Those are the people who end up being successful. The people who go out there and work the numbers—people who are willing to hear no and keep going. This ability is infinitely more important than your intelligence level.

How High Is <u>Your</u> Failure Quotient?

So, how much failure can *you* endure on the road to success?

How much negative feedback can *you* experience before it starts to get to you?

How many errors and mistakes are *you* willing to make in order to achieve extraordinary success?

These are not just rhetorical questions. The answers to these questions are key indicators as to whether you will achieve outrageous success and get everything you want in life...

Or simply settle for crumbs.

The key thing to keep in mind is that no one will remember your failures, only your successes.

There's a long list of products, inventions, and discoveries that happened as a direct result of failed projects and botched experiments. For example: Jell-O, shatterproof glass, the microwave oven, the Walkman, Levi jeans, Band-Aids, Kleenex, corn flakes, popsicles, penicillin—all of these are what inventors lovingly refer to as happy mistakes—and the list goes on and on.

The tires you drive on are the result of a bungled experiment by Charles Goodyear—the unintended result of which turned out to be vulcanized rubber.

Coca-Cola's renaissance and rebirth is the direct result of their "New Coke" debacle.

In an interview, Dr. Robert Schuller said: "The Crystal Cathedral was the result of my inability to find a hall to start a church."

And did you ever wonder how the model T got its name? Because Henry Ford had already gone through Models A–S.

All of these inventions were the result of something tried and failed. In fact, Silicon Valley is a veritable graveyard of mistakes—of things tried and failed. Yet the case can be made that failure *is* Silicon Valley's greatest strength. Because in Silicon Valley they have decided that failure is <u>not</u> a taboo. It is a rite of passage.

Brian Carruthers

When I began my career in network marketing, I knew I had found my path to success in life. I fell in love. But can you imagine the feeling when you go introduce your newfound love to your family and friends, and they tell you they don't like her?

That is devastating. My family told me I was wasting my time with that "little home based business thing" and encouraged me to quit.

It's not like they just said NO to the opportunity for themselves to join me, but they went farther and advised me to quit. But I knew what I knew, and I was sold out on my vision of where I was headed. I could not let any dream stealers divert me. As I made 200 phone calls in my first 3 days in the business to everyone I could think of, 184 of them told me NO. That's one hundred and eighty-four rejections, if you want to call it that.

But you see, that's not how I looked at it. I was taught to look at it like a sorting process, and I was only looking for the lookers. If one in ten might join my business and partner with me, then it was going to be a numbers game. I decided to go through the numbers faster than anyone else, with greater levels of passion, enthusiasm and urgency.

So I sorted 184 of the 200 out, and 16 said YES and started in the business with me. It was from these initial seeds that my empire sprung up. As they say, "You can always count the number of seeds in an apple, but you can never count the number of apples in a seed."

I am so proud of myself, frankly, for not letting the initial NO's that I encountered knock me out of the box of my lifetime opportunity. Many people cannot say that. The world is full of starters, but few finishers. I was determined to finish and win. Every day I would get on the phone and call, call, call – inviting people to presentations, to conference calls, to review information. I made the routine a habit. I found that success is a habit, it doesn't just happen.

I broke my 27-year old company records of going to the top Platinum level in a mere six months, and being the quickest to earn a million dollars. I was on a mission and doing great. I recruited my stock broker into the business. He was a young guy just like me, and he was on track to be a super star. He had the skills, being able to speak well, looked successful, and was hungry. We worked together for about a year and built up a good team. He was on his way, and my mentors said they thought he was destined to be the next me.

Can you imagine the feeling? I was so pumped.

But one day I opened the front door of my house to get the mail, and I almost tripped over a big box of company videos and material with a note on top that read: "You can have these, I'm done."

He had a few home meetings one week where nobody showed up, and he got frustrated and quit. I was devastated. How could he quit? We had invested so much time to get things to where they were, and he was going to be a top earner.

I felt like quitting myself, for about a few days. I learned a lesson in this. Just like I sort through prospects to find distributors, I also must sort through distributors to find the leaders who will stick around long enough to achieve greatness. The good news is that I went on from this blow to my morale by reminding myself that I was doing this business for me (and for those who want to win) and not for him. I went on to build even bigger, to where my team was recruiting over 6000 new people and over 22,000 new customers... a MONTH.

A NO cannot be allowed to infect our vision, nor can a quitter.

- Brian Carruthers, #1 Recruiter in Network Marketing, Trainer, Author of Building an Empire, www.BrianCarruthers.com

Mining for Gold ("The Need for Speed")

In the early days, gold could be found by sifting in rivers with shallow metal pans—hence the phrase "panning for gold." This went on for years until virtually all the exposed gold had been collected.

Eventually, however, the process shifted from looking for gold on the ground to looking for gold *in* the ground. The process involves:

- Digging shafts in the ground with large machinery
- Removing millions of pounds of large rocks, quartz, dirt, and debris
- Pulverizing the rocks with heavy iron crushers called "stamps" to find the gold

Eventually, even this gave way to hydraulic mining, where pressurized water is used to blast away hillsides. The soil from the hillside runs down into a valley where the silt and water can be separated.

What's most interesting about the most modern of these methods is that—while the goal is to find gold—at no time during the process are the miners looking for gold.

They're simply removing dirt.

What anyone who has ever mined for gold will readily tell you is that—if you're looking for gold while you're mining gold, you'll go mad.

Why?

Because there is so little gold.

The most effective way to mine gold is not to look for gold. It's to remove everything around it that isn't gold.

Remove the dirt.
Find the gold.

The difference between success and failure in mining (meaning making money) is not just the removal of the dirt—it's how quickly and cost-effectively the dirt is removed.

Thomas Edison and the Need to "Fail Faster"

One of the greatest examples during the twentieth century of someone who not only had a high NO-Quotient but also understood the need for speed when it came to failing was Thomas Edison.

Edison, as you know, engaged himself in a lifelong, relentless pursuit of the invention of the incandescent light bulb. And, as the story goes—after Edison's ten-thousandth failed attempt— a reporter asked how it felt to have failed ten thousand times.

Edison replied: "Dear man, you misunderstand. I have not failed at all. I have successfully discovered ten thousand ways that do not work."

But here's what is even more interesting.

At one point, Edison hired additional inventors to work in his Menlo Park studio, knowing full well they were inferior to him in terms of their ability. So why did he do it?

So he could fail faster.

Edison was often referred to by his nickname, The Wizard of Menlo Park. But, just like with the *Wizard of Oz*, when the curtain was pulled back the "wizard" was nothing more than an ordinary man with an extraordinary failure quotient.

And, as a result, an ordinary man did an extraordinary thing— he failed his way to success—and literally lit the world.

Quantity Trumps Quality

Now, we don't want to discount the importance of a quality presentation when it comes to influencing others and achieving success. But the reality is that:

- The number of doors you knock on...
- The number of people you approach and invite...

- The number of shots you take...

In other words, the number of presentations you make is *significantly more important* than how perfectly you do them.

The quality of the presentation is not the critical factor. The critical factor was that a presentation took place. *Period.*

Think of it this way:

Sometimes the worst approach will end in a yes because even the worst presentation in the world still has a chance to be successful if what you have available to offer is of value and interest to the prospect—especially compared to the perfect presentation that is never delivered.

Ray Higdon's Take...

Quantity vs. Quality

The question as to which is more important—the quantity of presentations you make versus the quality of those presentations—is of great fascination to me. Let's touch on quality first.

For most of my life, until maybe ten years ago, I was terrified of getting up in front of any size group and speaking. Now, I've been blessed to have spoken in front of 15,000 people. What's interesting is how many people comment on what a natural speaker I am—which is kind of funny. They didn't see all the sleepless nights I spent terrified of the speech I had to give the next day.

Ultimately, the only way I was able to get comfortable and look natural in front of an audience was to regularly speak in front of an audience. It wasn't from the time spent prepping for it.

When my wife and I ended up becoming the top income earners in our network marketing company, we did a lot of presentations. Some of them were pretty good. But a lot of them weren't all that fantastic and that was okay. We got where we wanted to be by doing a lot of presentations, so I can tell you first hand, the quantity of presentations you do is without a doubt more important than quality—especially in a network marketing space.

The problem with a lot of people in network marketing is that they feel they must perfect and hone their presentation prior to actually doing it. That's one of the biggest problems in network marketing and the entrepreneurial space—how people suffer from the disease of perfectionism. People want to perfect the script or the follow-up before going out there and presenting it to the world.

Chasing perfect quality can be very, very dangerous when it comes to being an entrepreneur or a network marketer.

Here's what's interesting, though. If you walk into an appliance store, the salesperson's goal is to sell you a fridge, right? But in network marketing, we're not selling our product or an opportunity. We're selling others on their own ability to replicate what we're doing. We're convincing them they have what it takes to build a business—and that's unique.

For example: I once recruited a guy who was earning a million dollars a year as a professional speaker. The dude was super polished. We had our first home meeting, and he came out in a suit and was super smooth. I can tell you it was an amazing presentation.

But no one joined.

Why? Because no one thought they could be as good as him. In his perfection, what he actually did was make everyone feel they could never replicate what he was doing at the front of the room.

When it comes to network marketing, I think perfect presentations can be detrimental to your goal. Perfection can be a bad thing, which is kind of unique to this profession.

Ironically, some of my very worst presentations have brought in some of my best people. As the saying goes, you can't say the wrong thing to the right person, or the right thing to the wrong person. In a lot of ways, I've found that to be true.

The only thing I don't like about that saying is that it kind of indicates you shouldn't even try to become a better speaker, which, of course, you should. You should consistently try to improve yourself, but that never happens by practicing in a room by yourself. Spending a hundred hours in a room by yourself, trying to develop the perfect presentation, is a waste of time.

Network marketing is fairly unique in that you can absolutely earn while you learn, and the chances of your first presentation being great are so slim and so unlikely—no matter how many hours you prepare—you're better off just going and getting it over with.

Just go do it.

The Insurance Sales Story

Years ago, there was an insurance company in Chicago that called in a consultant to analyze why their profits were declining. The company was averaging only two and a half sales per agent per month, and they were at wits end.

When the consultant arrived, he immediately put his finger on the problem. He told the company: "Your only problem is that your salespeople are not seeing enough prospects."

Well, this solution was way too simple for the top executives at the company—after all, they'd paid this consultant big money, and they wanted him to discover a big problem! So, when they complained, the consultant said: "Fine. I'll prove it to you."

The consultant took a group of the company's salespeople, a cross-section of the salesforce from best to worst, and told them they were to start selling policies door to door in neighborhoods where they didn't know a soul. There would be no leads provided to them. There was no qualifying of prospects. They were to knock on doors and—when the homeowner answered—they *must* start the sales presentation by saying:

"You don't want to buy insurance, do you?"

Their mission was to see how many people they could repeat that message to every day. That was it. Needless to say, the salespeople were a bit skeptical. But the results spoke volumes.

Fifty-nine out of every sixty homeowners they approached said, "You're right! I don't want to buy insurance. Get lost!"

But...

<u>One</u> out of every sixty said, "As a matter of fact, I do need insurance. Come on in."

On the surface, one out of sixty doesn't seem like a very good closing ratio. And it wouldn't be if it took two weeks to eliminate the fifty-nine that did not want insurance. But this isn't a story about closing ratios.

It's a story about speed.

The key to the program's success was the speed at which the salespeople disqualified and eliminated prospects who did not want or need their product (the non-buyers) to get to the one out of sixty that did.

It's a story about removing dirt to find gold—and to do it quickly and cheaply enough to make a profit.

Jordan Adler

Up until this point, I'd never had success in any network marketing company or any personal business.

I met a guy who told me that in the business of recruiting you need to be prepared to sign-up 20-30 people to find one, what he called, "a big hitter" and he said that you can't change the numbers. If you're talking to a real-estate broker, if you're talking to an insurance broker, or if you're talking to a top network marketer, they'll all tell you: "To find one "big hitter" you need to be prepared to sign up 20-30 people."

I was living in a rental in Old Town Tempe paying $200 a month. I took a black marker and I drew a grid on the wall – 100 squares, 10 x 10. In that company, I needed to find 20 customers, so I wrote in big black letters above the grid, "Find 20," and then I wrote, "Have fun," next to the "Find 20," because I wasn't having fun. I had bill collectors after me, and I had 22 credit cards with $36,000 in debt, and at my job, they had just cut my pay in half.

The top position in the company was Executive Director, and so at the bottom of the grid I wrote, "ED," for Executive Director. I was single and dating so if I eventually invited a lady over the first thing we'd do is take a tour of the house and she'd get to the bedroom, and see this grid over the bed that said "Have fun," at the top, and then "Find 20," and then down at the bottom it said "ED," for Executive Director. Rather shocked, she wanted to know, "What on earth does this mean?" Well, I would write dates in these boxes every time I would give a presentation.

My goal was to do three presentations a week, 12 a month, knowing that probably 11 of them would say no, and my goal was to sign-up one person a month for two years.

I was going to find and sign-up one person a month for two years, do 12 presentations a month, three a week on my lunches, every single week regardless of what anybody said to me.

It didn't matter if they were negative, or if they were angry, or if they were happy, or if they were complacent, or interested, I was going to do 12 presentations a month for two years, knowing that if I did that I'd probably sponsor 20-30 people. I signed up 19 people in two years.

My 19th person I signed up was a lady in New Mexico who led me to over 12,000 distributors and over 40,000 customers, and it made me my first $1,000,000.

- Jordan Adler, The $20 Million Network Marketer, www.JordanAdler.com

Contrary to what you've been told, opportunity does not knock.

<u>You</u> knock.

Opportunity answers.

Unfortunately, when it answers, it often says...

Your emotional reaction in that moment will have a profound impact on the quality of every aspect of your life.

Your Emotional Reaction to
YES and NO

According to the teachings of Aristotle, there are three main elements that influence our thoughts and actions. These elements are:

ETHOS.

LOGOS.

PATHOS.

Ethos has to do with character, as in the word *ethical*.

Logos has to do with reason, like in the word *logical*.

And then there's pathos.

Pathos has to do with emotion—as in *passion*.

Hopefully with all that we've covered you've begun the process of changing your mental perspective regarding success and failure. And yes and no. If you haven't, it might be more than your perspective. It's probably something deeply rooted in your emotions.

Your pathos.

For example, here is another concept that might be somewhat counter-intuitive to what you currently believe—and perhaps everything you've ever been taught.

To be effective in virtually any endeavor, you need to have <u>less</u> pathos, not more.

In other words, to be *less* emotionally connected to the outcome of the interaction.

To be clear, we're not talking about zero passion—but probably less passion than you're feeling *(your <u>internal</u> emotion)* and showing to your prospects *(your <u>external</u> emotion)*.

When we say less passion, consider the example of a surgeon who must remain unemotional and somewhat dispassionate to conduct surgery. It's not that doctors should be completely dispassionate, but make no mistake: a certain amount of calm, levelheaded detachment is required to be effective.

In fact, doctors aren't usually allowed to operate on relatives or loved ones. Why? Because they are too close and too emotional to remain detached enough to focus on the job at hand.

And the same is true for us as salespeople. Our attachment to outcomes tends to make us too emotional—*and less effective.*

Your reaction to hearing

YES and NO

should be of equal emotional intensity.

The ultimate place you can get to is where hearing yes and no contain the same emotional charge.

Ray Higdon's Take...

On Going to Your "Warm Market"

My overarching thought is that you should only go to your warm market when you don't care if they'll join or not.

If going to your warm market—your mother, father, brother-in-law, sister, aunt, uncle, cousin, son, whatever—has a 0.001 percent chance of getting you frustrated or upset if they say no, then hold off until there's no chance you'll be negatively affected. When that's the case, go to them. Until then, avoid them.

Now, don't get me wrong. I'm not saying you should only focus on strangers who don't know you or that you should never bother with your warm market. I'm just suggesting you wait until you don't care if they sign-up or not.

Treating YES and NO the Same

The critical thing is to reach a place where you can hear yes and no with the same emotional reaction—in the neutral zone.

Now, we understand there will always be some part of us that will be happier when a prospect says yes. After all, *yes* pays the bills. That, and we're human.

The goal is to reach a point where the elation of hearing yes and the deflation of hearing no are minimized—even if our internal reactions can't be eliminated entirely.

Anyone can be happy and positive when things are going their way. That's easy. The question is: How do you respond when the going gets tough? When things don't go the way you'd like. When you hear no.

In poker they have a term for the emotional reaction players have after a few bad hands, or what they call a bad beat. It's called:

"Going on tilt."

It's easy for card players to stay levelheaded and in control when they're playing well and luck is going their way. But the difference between the best and the rest of the pack is your ability to control your emotions when things *aren't* going their way.

The best players must train themselves to avoid going on tilt.

And so do you.

When things don't go your way—especially for an extended period of time—you must learn to control your emotions and keep yourself from going on tilt.

Here's a great example:

The St. Louis Cardinals defeated the Detroit Tigers in the 2006 World Series. One of the noteworthy things from that series was the performance of Cardinal shortstop David Eckstein.

In Eckstein's first eleven plate appearances, he was 0-11. His first hit in the series didn't come until late in the third game.

But then he got eight hits in his next eleven at bats—winding up eight for twenty-two, with a 0.364 batting average—and was named World Series MVP.

Even when things looked bad—when they *were* bad—Eckstein managed to keep his emotions in check. He did not allow himself to go on tilt.

It's critical that we do not climb aboard the yes-no emotional rollercoaster, where every yes has us celebrating—and every no drives us into a downward cycle of emotional thoughts and ineffective actions.

It's a very difficult cycle to escape.

One top sales performer described his mental visioning process of selling this way: His territory was a large house with many rooms. Each room was filled with prospects, which were imaginary objects like lamps and toys and dishes. On the bottom of each object was a label that read:

"YES"

or

"NO"

His job as a salesperson, he said, was to walk into the room, pick up an object and read the label. If it said no, he put it back down. If it said yes, he took it back to the office with him.

His approach was to sell without pathos and not take no personally. It is this type of emotional detachment that keeps no from being personal.

No isn't personal.

The Jerry Kosinski Book Experiment

It has long been thought that most New York publishing houses do not give serious consideration to unsolicited manuscripts. So author Chuck Ross decided to find out if it was true that most manuscripts were rejected without ever being read.

Using an assumed name, Ross re-typed the best-selling, national award-winning book *Steps* by Jerry Kosinski, which had been published by Random House and had already sold over four hundred thousand copies—a mega-success by any standard. He submitted the re-typed manuscript to twenty-eight publishing houses and literary agents, including Random House and others who had previously published titles by Kosinski.

All twenty-eight rejected the work.

Including Random House!

Most simply sent the standard rejection letter. But one publisher sent a personal note:

> *"Upon review of the manuscript, Jerry Kosinski comes to mind, but on the whole the writing wasn't in Kosinski's league."*

Ross had proved his point. Most manuscripts were rejected out-of-hand, with little or no regard to the quality of the work.

Our point in sharing this story is that the quality of the book meant nothing to most publishers or agents. And, as such, one rejection letter—or a thousand—often says nothing about a book or a product or a service.

What it says something about is the people rejecting it.

Question: What if the real Jerry Kosinski had taken his early rejections as fact and stopped submitting his manuscript for consideration?

The reality is that seven out of ten times a rejection of your product, service, and/or idea—*has nothing to do with you or the quality of your product, service, or idea!*

In other words, no isn't personal.

And often times it isn't very educated either.

Admittedly, for many people adopting this attitude is easier said than done. And reaching the point where you can detach yourself—and whatever it is you're selling—requires a lot of personal programming.

Or, more accurately, *reprogramming*.

If hearing no has been a challenge for you in the past—or perhaps still is—then you've got some work to do on your thinking and how you process rejection.

One of the side benefits of selling with less outward emotion is that others are often more drawn to the offer precisely because of the lack of concern for the outcome. Conversely, too much outward passion is often interpreted as desperation.

As one top sales performer said: "I tell the story of our product in simple, unemotional, unbiased terms, and make the case why the customer should invest. Then I lean back and wait. Anything I do beyond that is usually counter-productive."

This brings us to one of the most important things we hope you will take away from this book. It's an amazingly easy-to-remember concept made up of two letters repeated four times—and should become the mantra of anyone who faces rejection on a regular basis.

You may be familiar with it:

SW-SW-SW-SW

Some Will.

Some Won't.

So What?

Someone's Waiting.

You've just made a presentation, and the prospect said yes.

Good. No matter what you're selling, *some will* say yes.

Or they said no.

Okay. *Some won't.*

No matter what you're selling—regardless of how poorly or how well you presented the offer—some people are going to say no to you.

So what?

Accept the idea that no is a perfectly acceptable answer. It may not be the answer you want, but if that's what the prospect says, be okay with it. In most cases, the no has nothing to do with you, so don't take it personally. Brush it off. Move on. Because:

Someone's waiting.

There's always someone else who wants—and perhaps desperately needs—exactly what you have to offer.

That's why it's important to have a good solid list of prospects in your pipeline. The more potential prospects you have to turn to in your pipeline, the less the impact will be on your emotions.

There was a time, early in our business, when finances were tight. Then we got a call from the only prospect we had in the pipeline at the time, and we remember holding our breath until she said, "Yes, we'd like to hire you to speak at our upcoming convention."

We were so relieved.

It just so happened that a friend was in town, so we all went out to lunch and celebrated, followed by us picking up the tab. Then we got back to our office and saw the flashing light on the telephone answering machine. We pushed the button and heard the same woman telling us they had just cancelled the meeting.

There are few times in our business lives that we remember feeling as sick as we did right then. In that moment, we vowed to never have so few deals in the pipeline.

When your possibilities are few and far between, each possibility takes on enormous significance. That is not what you want. If you have too much riding on one deal, one prospect, one interview, one audition, one idea, one meeting, one presentation, one speech—*one anything*—then you will invariably suffer greater anxiety about the outcome.

You must have enough irons in the fire to ensure that one disappointment does not devastate you and put you on tilt.

And if you do have an emotional reaction to any one situation, make it just that—*a single situation*. What happened during the last call, meeting, conversation, audition, or submission has absolutely nothing to do with the next one. What is past is past. The rejection from the people who said no five weeks ago, five days ago—or five minutes ago—should have nothing to do with the presentation you're going to make five minutes from now.

Unless you let it.

There is no carry-over effect (or at least there shouldn't be) unless *you* carry it over.

Remember: The next prospect deserves your best presentation. But how can you deliver your best presentation to the *next* prospect if you're still on tilt over the *last* one?

Onyx Coale

Over the years, prior to me joining network marketing, I had been pitched on, what feels like, every network marketing company. I never agreed to sit down and see a presentation. But everybody I knew in network marketing was saying, "Try my product," and "Do this business opportunity."

Every time I saw anybody coming near me who was a network marketer, I would turn around and run! My mind was saying, "I don't want to have anything to do with you. No! No! No! No!" For years this was how I felt about network marketing. Finally, I was approached by the parents of the young woman who was babysitting my children.

It was interesting, because they had what so many people lacked. They never accepted "no" as an answer. They just kept coming back around to me.

They also knew I would love their product, because it was a healthcare product. I'm very much into my health. I believe in investing in health to avoid health issues rather than waiting until you are dealing with real health challenges. They knew I would be passionate about the product.

The first time they invited me I said no. The second time they invited me I said no.

Then they came by on their boat. We lived on the same lake. I saw them coming. I went running inside. Here I was hiding again. Then, of course, they brought me over the product. I thanked them, tucked it under the kitchen counter, and never even tried it.

Later they called me, and they changed their approach.

They said, "Onyx, we really value your opinion, please, would you come and have a look at what we got ourselves into?"

I knew if I didn't go, they would never leave me alone! So I went to the meeting.

The smart girl that I am, I decided I was going to leave my checkbook at home, because they weren't going to catch me.

There were 30 people in the room. It was the first time in my life I actually saw someone draw the circles. The guy presenting was making $8,000 a week. He'd been in the industry for many years, but he'd been in this particular company for eight months.

By the way, I am a single mom of three girls. As I'm watching the presentation, I'm thinking to myself, "You can't make money unless you help other people make money? I like this!"

They started talking about the product. They talked about the opportunity. Everything started to connect and go ding, ding, ding, ding! I knew I was at the right place. That was the point I finally said yes.

It was the sixth time they asked me that I finally said yes. Now I have had lots of my own distributors who experience people saying, "No!" I say, you know — as we all know — so what? They are saying no right now. They are not saying no to you. They haven't mortally wounded you. Your life is not over.

Take a deep breath. Come back around again, because time and circumstances changes everything for everybody.

- Onyx Coale, #1 Female MLM Earner, Consultant and Speaker

Ray Higdon's Take...

Not Taking NO Personally

Here's my take on the fear of rejection: It's a sign that you're placing a higher value on your fear of looking bad in front of other people than you are on making an impact in someone else's life. It's saying, "I place a higher value on how I look than I do on impacting other's lives and making a difference on this planet." No one wants to hear that because it's tough. It's tough love.

The truth is if you're not willing to practice getting rejected so you can develop the ability to go out and prospect for your network marketing opportunity, that's fine. Just own it. Embrace it. Seriously, it's okay.

Many people take the less confrontational path, of course. They get normal jobs and snap themselves into society's system. They follow the traditional path. They rarely ever get rejected. They rarely ever face criticism. They rarely ever have to worry about looking good in front of an audience. They may not like their lives. They may not have the kind of results that they want in their life. But they've decided it's more important to play it safe than to face rejection.

There was a time when, if someone rejected me, I would go home and eat a bunch of ice cream and feel sorry for myself. Getting past the tendency to take rejection personally takes practice. It really does.

Learning not to take rejection personally isn't something you hear one time and, poof, you're vaccinated from the rejection virus. It just doesn't happen.

The way that you get past rejection is to get out there and start getting rejected!

When I was in real estate, I read many books on negotiating, and one of the books said that most people are nervous about negotiating and they just need more practice. The suggestion in the book was to go to a yard sale, pick a table of stuff that you don't want, and start negotiating.

Find a table with twenty dollars worth of stuff on it and say, "Hey, I'll give you two bucks for everything on that table." Now, what's going to happen? More than likely they're going to say, "No!" Then you say, "Okay, well how about $2.50." And they say, "No!" And so on.

The way you get past rejection is to go out and actually practice getting past rejection—by experiencing rejection, not by thinking about it or telling yourself not to take it personally. You get past the negative feelings about rejection by allowing yourself to be rejected.

If you're a single guy, maybe you go out there and ask for phone numbers. Maybe you're asking for a date and that's how you're more comfortable getting rejected. But you need to get out there and start getting rejected.

I've had people who were so stricken with the paralysis of their fear of rejection that I told them: "Hey, go get a telemarketing job. You probably won't last more than a week, but, in the short amount of time you'll be there, you'll probably get to experience lots of rejection."

When I was in telemarketing, we made 450 calls a day, and if you got thirty sales you were one of the top salespeople in the entire company. So if you calculate that out to be a full week, that's 450 dials a day multiplied by five—we're talking 2,250 calls—most of which involved rejection. But if you're making a few sales here and there, you'll also start to make the connection between rejections and sales. Rejection and money. Rejection and success.

One of the best examples in the world is being a waiter or waitress. Here's someone who serves people all day long, and in every case they get to say: "Hey, would you like to see a dessert menu?" I'm willing to bet that at least 50 percent of the time, maybe more, people say, "No, thanks."

Here's what's interesting. The waiter or waitress doesn't get all bent out of shape when people say no. Now, why is that? It's because they have no connection to the outcome. They don't equate someone turning down the key lime pie as some kind of attack on their self-image.

Neither should you.

I want you to fully understand that there was a time when I took rejection personally and felt devastated by it. But I developed my courage muscle. I developed my skill and ability to handle rejection.

Very few people on the planet are born rejection-proof. They develop it. They build it. Just like no one's born with humongous biceps—they have to work the muscles and develop them. In the same way, you develop your rejection muscle by doing whatever you can to start hearing no more often.

I can tell you that at this point—because of the skills I have developed—you could hook up a heart monitor to me and have fifty people tell me no, and my heart rate won't change a bit. Why? Because I have no connection to the outcome—I literally just don't care. It doesn't mean I don't care about the person, just that I am infinitely more focused on the process than the result.

There are a lot of times where I'll shoot a training video that barely gets any shares or comments. That's okay. Because the next day, I'm just going to wake up and do another one. Getting the practice in every day, getting past that fear of rejection, that's the key.

Tupac Derenoncourt

I was actually prompted to look for an alternative income stream during the softening of the economy, right before 'the great recession.' A good friend of mine piqued my interest about the company that I'm involved with. He had been able to retire two household incomes and was a home Dad at that time. I said, "Wow, show me how to do this!"

In network marketing your initial marketing plan really is to share the opportunity with friends and family, and there comes a time where you feel like you've told everybody. I always joke with people that it takes me three years now to recruit somebody.

People say, "Three years? Well, that doesn't make sense." Well, once you've had your initial success and you've talked to everybody, then it takes a longer time because people feel like they've missed it, or like you were lucky—all these different things and stories they make up in their head.

There was one particular young lady that I knew for a few years. Prior to getting involved we were in the same industry. She lived in Philadelphia. I called her up and I sent her to a meeting. I said, "Hey, I kind of shifted. I want you to take a look at what I'm doing. I think you would be incredible at it."

She went to the meeting with two friends and I found out later they stood up in the middle of the meeting and left. So, I followed up with her and she said, "It started late and we had something to do. It seemed okay, but, not for us." I said, "Okay, cool, no problem." Fast-forward six months. I called her and I said, "Hey, I'm telling you, you'd be great at this. You need to take a look at it."

I sent her to one of our company's regional events. I checked in with one of my team members and said, "How did it go today?" They said, "Oh, it was great." Then I found out that everyone was out at Dave & Busters.

So, I thought I would give her a call and see if she would meet about this one more time. I invited her out to Dave & Busters and she says, "Oh sure, I love Dave & Busters."

She comes out to Dave & Busters, and she's like, "Man, everyone is paying with these company cards..." because it was a team event after the main event, and she's seeing all of this and says, "I'm interested now." It just so happens that she falls into that 'dolphin' category where social events are more her thing, in her comfort zone. And so, when she went, she was kind of open at that point.

Ultimately it took her three years to get involved. If it wasn't for keeping that drip going—to have kept following-up and inviting her—she wouldn't have joined.

Three years in, she became Philadelphia's first female senior vice president in the entire company.

- Tupac Derenoncourt, Top Network Marketing Professional, Multi-Million Dollar Earners Club, www.TupacD.com

A Heightened Sense of NO-Awareness™

Here's a question for you:

How many times did you hear the word *no* yesterday? Last week? Last month? What's the total for the year? Do you know?

If not, it's time for you to start counting every no you hear because the very act of counting them increases your NO-Awareness. And this, in turn, will enhance your ability to go for no.

To do this effectively, you need a process or system for counting the number of noes you hear. The most formal device would be a hand-held counter, which can be found online. But these are not necessary and, quite frankly, we find them bulky and impractical to use unless you're a telemarketer sitting at a desk and out-of-sight of the customer.

Instead, we suggest using the very effective process created by W. Clement Stone.

W. Clement Stone, founder and president of Combined Insurance Company of America, was one of the greatest businessmen and philanthropists of the twentieth century. He was also the original publisher of *SUCCESS* magazine and author of some of the most important self-help books ever written—including *Success Through a Positive Mental Attitude* and *The Success System That Never Fails*.

But, more than anything, W. Clement Stone was a salesman— and proud of it.

Stone had an interesting and effective technique for helping new salespeople get over their fear of rejection. When training new salespeople, he would have them put twenty dry beans in one of their pockets. To keep them from getting discouraged, he would tell them: "When you get a no from a prospect, move a bean from one pocket to the other. I promise that before all twenty beans have been moved, you'll get a sale."

And he was usually right.

Now you could just keep track in a notebook. Right? Sure. But placing the beans (or glass stones that can be bought from a crafts store like Michaels) in your pocket serves as a reminder to go for no throughout the day.

Also, many people tell us the stones turn selling into more of a game as opposed to a task—making the process fun and reminding them not to take the process so seriously.

That is what selling should be, right?

It should be a game.

Whatever method you decide to use, you must put a process in place for counting the noes you receive.

To Value NO, You Must Know Its Value

One of the most powerful approaches to enjoy hearing no is to calculate the dollar value of each no you obtain. This is done by taking the total value of all your sales or production over a given period of time—the longer the period, the better (and more accurate)—and dividing that amount by the total number of noes and yeses it took to achieve it.

To illustrate the concept, consider this story:

In 1967 Allen Breed began offering the airbag sensors he invented to Detroit automakers, but the big three automakers told him to get lost. They weren't interested in such an expensive item they perceived as unnecessary.

But Breed didn't go away.

Not only did Allen Breed keep pestering the automakers, but he also invested huge quantities of time and money lobbying Congress. Finally, almost twenty years after he started, Congress passed legislation mandating the use of airbags. But it still took another ten years before his first sale was made. It wasn't until 1995—almost thirty years after Breed's first rejection—that Breed Technologies, now Key Safety Systems, made its first big sale.

And we do mean big.

The sale was for 23 million airbag sensors—for a net profit of $120 million.

Now here's the question: Did Allen Breed earn $120 million in 1995 when the automakers finally said yes? Or did he earn $4.2 million a year for every year he was willing to hear no?

Admittedly, this is an extreme example. So, let's take it down to a typical, day-to-day scenario that is a little more relatable.

Mary traditionally closes one out of every five presentations she makes, with an average sale worth $500 in commission. Dividing the $500 Mary earns in commission by the total of all calls—in this case five—the four noes and the one yes—we determine that every time Mary makes a presentation, she makes $100:

Regardless of the outcome.

In this way, neither yes nor no has a greater value than the other.

You may be familiar with this idea already. But even if you've heard it before, there are three things we know:

One:

Even if you have heard it, chances are good that you've never actually taken the time to calculate the value of every no you've heard...

Two:

Even if you do know the value, you probably don't think about it every time you hear no, and...

Three:

Even if you are consciously thinking about the value every time you hear no, you are almost assuredly not verbalizing it out loud to yourself.

And *verbalize it* you should—at least if you're going to begin valuing it, that is.

Now, let's be clear: We're not talking about verbalizing it out loud in front of a prospect (though we've actually run into a few people who do!)

Do it when you're alone after a meeting—or right after hanging up the phone—and say:

"Thanks for the $____."

Whether the answer was yes or no doesn't matter.

Because that's the point.

Lisa Jimenez

"I'm frustrated!" I said to my upline. "All these Nos are really getting to me."

He smiled as if he were holding back a secret.

"Whaaaaaat?" I yelled, wanting to smack the smile off his face.

"Lisa, you just haven't learned the key to accepting all those Nos." he replied as he went into this explanation about law of average, stats, and numbers. I didn't understand all of it but what I did hear was, "So the fact is... you make $500 on every No that you're willing to hear."

Well, that was a vision I could wrap my head around!

He explained to me that if I can deal with 7-10 no's, I will inevitably get a yes. And that one yes will yield more than $5000 a month over the course of my career. I divided the $5000 by 10 and saw I make $500 off every no. So, for the next few months I pasted a hundred-dollar bill on my phone to train my brain that every no was a hundred dollars multiplied by five!

Every time I picked it up and made a cold-call or any kind of prospecting call and received a "no" – no matter how friendly or harsh - it was like, ah, thanks for the $500. As soon as I hung up the phone I'd shout, "Thanks for the five hundred bucks!"

Very soon, I had transformed my mindset about the word "no," and receiving – notice the language, receiving a "no" as a privilege of making $500.

Really, it's all about transforming our relationship to the word "no," and transforming our relationship to rejection. Your ability to change the meaning of no is where you make the most money.

A lot of people are more committed to looking good than they are to accepting the reality to our business model. When you are less committed to looking good and more committed to being willing to mess up, be nervous, look silly, manage your emotions, and deal with receiving noes, you'll become rich and help others to do the same!

What about you?

Are you more committed to looking good than getting rich?

Are you more committed to feeling confident than helping others get rich?

Give yourself permission to retrain your brain around what it really takes to max out your company comp plan; what it really takes to help yourself and others create a radical difference in their financial freedom! Do the internal work to retrain your brain around the word no; realizing that's where the money is; and even more importantly, that's where the growth is!

Just imagine the person you will become when you train your brain to accept a no (and the five hundred bucks that no will generate!) and expand who you show up to be in the world.

While that process takes time and intention, it is just a process. That process has an end in sight. When the process of training your brain around receiving no's is complete, you will be a force of confidence; a walking talking vessel of faith!

And, we need more people like you on this planet!

- Lisa Jimenez M.Ed., Business Coach and Speaker, Author, Conquer Fear! and Slay the Dragon! www.Rx-Success.com

Having YES-Goals Are Important.
Having NO-Goals Are Critical.

In the beginning of this book, we suggested there would be certain concepts that would challenge your thinking. The next concept will definitely be one of them because we're going to suggest a somewhat radical change to the way you currently set goals.

And that radical change is this:

Beginning right now—today—start setting NO-Goals.

No, we're not suggesting you stop setting goals. Goals are important to success. Critical, in fact.

We're talking about setting a goal for the number of times you intend to hear the word *no* (in other words, a failure quota) in addition to having a goal for the number of times you hear the word *yes* (a success quota).

The problem with focusing exclusively on YES-Goals is what tends to happen when we reach (or even get close to reaching) the goal we've set for ourselves...

We slow down.

We begin to reward ourselves for our success. But how do we reward ourselves? By shutting down the activities that led to our success in the first place.

The question is: why?

Why does our productivity often come to a screeching halt? It's because of the insidious comfort zone.

Ray Higdon's Take...

Setting the NO-Goal of Twenty Noes Per Day

When I started setting NO-Goals for myself, I decided to go out and get twenty noes every day. Why? Where did the arbitrary number of twenty noes come from? Honestly, I think I picked twenty because there was no one around to tell me how unreasonable that was!

When I was eighteen or nineteen, I was a telemarketer, and we were selling long-distance services. It wasn't unheard of to make 450 calls a day. No network marketer I've ever met in my life makes even two hundred calls a day, right? But here we were making 450 calls a day—and there were a few people who did even more than that.

So getting twenty noes a day in my network marketing business seemed reasonable. Of course, I learned pretty quickly how tough that really was. And that hardly anyone has a number that high. I just didn't know.

The interesting thing is I've shared that story for years and years now, and I've yet to have anyone in the tens of thousands of people I've spoken to come to me and say, "Hey Ray, I did your plan. I got twenty noes a day."

So. I don't know. I guess I just wanted to push myself. That, or I simply did it out of ignorance. Sometimes I would hit the twenty no-goal in the afternoon. I don't believe there was a day that it took me more than three hours, at least I don't recall one.

The important thing to me was it worked.

Pat Petrini

When I first got started with network marketing, I was a 22-year old kid with big goals and no experience, but a willingness to do whatever it took to get there.

Like all "advantages in disguise," being young came with its own set of challenges. My mentor was coaching me to follow a "quality over quantity" approach in terms of the people that I talked to about the business, but the highest-caliber people in my network often didn't take me seriously.

On top of that, most of my friends had very different priorities than I did at the time. While I had dreams of building a large income and traveling the world on it, most of them were happy with getting a job, going to school and partying on the weekends.

While you could easily refer to these challenges as the disadvantages of trying to build a network marketing business when you are young, the truth is that all disadvantages are actually the doorway to powerful advantages if you are persistent enough to push through them.

My challenges proved to be no different.

With a lot of persistence, a lot of time on the phone, a lot of coffee shop gatherings and a lot of hotel meetings, I eventually worked my residual income up to around $1,000 per month. That's not an amazing figure by any means, but it is enough to change the lives of most people.

Now I had some proof. I was making some money. That allowed me to go back to the people that had originally told me "no" and say "hey, by the way, this thing is working!"

Some of them joined and some of them didn't.

Then my residual income grew to $2,500 per month. Again, I went back to the people that told me "no" and said "I'm just keeping you posted. This thing is working!"

As my income continued to grow, many of the people that didn't take me seriously at first started to take notice. It's not that they necessarily viewed me any differently, but a lot of them thought "if this kid can do this then I can definitely do it."

In that way, once I had built a bit of an income, my youth and inexperience started to actually work in my favor. My "disadvantage" had morphed into an "advantage!"

My income kept growing, and so did the allure of my story. And, as Jim Rohn often said, there is no better recruiting tool than a compelling story.

Eventually, I was making a healthy six-figure residual income, I was traveling the world and I was beginning to build wealth by investing much of my income. I was experiencing a level of freedom in my early twenties that most people will never experience in their entire lives.

Sometimes, it can be hard to see how our perceived disadvantages will ever work in our favor. They always do, though! In this way, advantages and disadvantages are really two sides of the same coin, and persistence is the path to the other side.

Persist!

- Pat Petrini, Network Marketing Speaker, Trainer, and Author of, The Miracle Morning for Network Marketers

The Perils of the Comfort Zone

To understand why so many people slow their performance when they reach their goals, we need to explore the nature of the comfort zone.

The term *comfort zone* was coined in the '60s by Jim Newman, who used the example of how heating and air conditioning works.

When someone sets a thermostat, they do it with the intent of creating a temperature comfort zone—say, from sixty-eight degrees on the low end to seventy-four degrees on the high end. Then, anytime the temperature in the room goes outside that range, the heat or air kicks on and returns the temperature within the comfort zone set.

Reality:

- Having a comfort zone is a very <u>GOOD</u> thing for controlling the temperature of a room.

- Having a comfort zone can be a very <u>BAD</u> thing when it comes to achieving maximum performance.

The problem is simple. When it comes to income and performance, we human beings have a system very similar to the system designed to control the temperature in a room. For example, if we need to make four sales a month to make the amount of money we need to live comfortably, we tend to work really hard to get those four sales.

That's the good part of the comfort zone.

The problem comes on the opposite end of the comfort spectrum. When our production is *greater* than we need to be comfortable, we shut the system down to remain in the comfort zone.

Sometimes this happens because we get lazy and would prefer not to keep pushing ourselves. Other times, it's because of the perception we have of our self-worth and ourselves.

In any case, the mere act of setting a yes-oriented quota will often—*consciously or unconsciously*—create the conditions for a self-fulfilling prophecy to occur. One only needs to look up the definition of the word *quota* to see the problem.

The dictionary defines a quota as:

> **"A proportional share," (which makes sense since everyone should be responsible for their proportional share) "the highest number or proportion."**

And there's the problem.

People tend to treat a quota as the highest number—the maximum, not the minimum. In other words, *the upper end of the comfort zone.*

That's the insidious thing about goals and quotas. They're intended to increase performance, yet they often end up limiting performance instead.

As the thirteenth-century Sufi poet and mystic Mevlana Rumi once said:

> *"If you are irritated by every rub, how will you ever become polished?"*

It is the friction of life that polishes us, and the risks we take—not simply our successes—that become the greatest measure of who we are.

Aaron Mathis

I feel like going for "no" has been my motto throughout my life. I've been told since I was young that I couldn't do this, I couldn't do that, and it never really deterred me. If anything, it just pushed me to prove them wrong.

My favorite 'Go for No' story is how my wife and I ended up together. Jessica and I have known each other since we were in 4th grade but we never really liked each other. We always kind of did our own thing, stayed in our own little cultures growing up. We graduated high school, went off, lived our own lives, and when I was 25 we ran into each other again.

I walked into the place where she was working. I started going in there frequently and something clicked in my head and I saw her in a different light. I asked her out, and I was told 'no,' but again that didn't deter me. After six months and saying 'no' at least two-dozen times she finally broke down - we went on a date. We went to a wedding together.

Ten months later we were married!

For the first several years of our marriage, Jessica was a server working the night shift. I was working for the City of Portland, working days, and Hailey, our daughter, was just a baby at the time. Our time together was literally passing Hailey off in the driveway as I was coming home and Jessica was going to work.

We were struggling financially trying to find an extra stream of income, and finding something that we could do from home that wasn't going to keep us away from each other even more was essential. We found network marketing through a product that we were already using and decided to engage in the business model. One of the very first things we were taught when we got into this industry is "no" means "not right now," and in the world that we live in, people's lives, and decisions, can change on a dime.

A lot of people will say "no" just because they're scared, but more than that, people who are a "no" today could be an "absolutely" tomorrow.

When people say "no" I just ask people if they're open to me coming back and following-up with them, checking in on them in a couple months, or if we have a new product, or if I have something else that I think they might be interested in, and usually people are open to that. I'll use a spreadsheet and put a date that I'm going to follow-up, a note of how the interaction went, and set the follow up date for whatever we determine that to be. Jessica's a pen and paper kind of girl; she's got notes. She's got rooms full of notes, but it works for her. I always tell people find a system that works for you and run with it.

One of the things that I find sad and a little scary about the world that we live in today is most people won't make a change until they're desperate, until they're forced to change. Most people aren't preparing for "what if," and with the world today, nobody's job is truly secure.

Unfortunately, the perception out there still today, even with thousands of growing successful companies in this industry, is that MLM is just either some cute little side business or it's a pyramid scheme. This industry is absolutely for real. The industrial age is over. The Information Age is here. Along with that, jobs are becoming more and more scarce, which means people are having to work independently, which opens the door to this amazing industry that we get to offer to others.

Jessica and I just celebrated 16 years of marriage, and this year marks a decade in this industry, with 8 of those years working our network marketing business together full-time from home. I feel so truly blessed that I adopted the "Go for No" mindset so early in my life. Employing that strategy has given me some of the most amazing things in my life, including the woman of my dreams, and a business that's building our dreams together.

- Aaron Mathis, Top Network Marketing Professional, www.facebook.com/jaaronmathis

Setting NO-Goals™

The immediate answer to the negative aspects of the comfort zone is to stop setting YES-Goals and set NO-Goals instead.

How does setting NO-Goals make the process different?

Let's take Jill for example.

Jill has had a great Monday. She went on three sales calls and closed them all, going three-for-three. Now, if Jill's quota is to make three sales for the week, what do you think is going to happen to the number of calls she's going to make over the next four days? We've got twenty bucks that says Jill slows down and significantly reduces the number of calls she makes.

In fact, another ten dollars says Jill ends the week with the same three sales she had on Monday afternoon. And in the blink of an eye, a great day has turned into an average week, all because Jill was operating with success quota rather than a failure quota.

The worst part is Jill just ended what is commonly referred to as a hot streak (and as Jerry Stafford sang in the '70s, "when you're hot, you're hot.")

It's amazing how many people will get on a hot streak—achieving a string of successes—only then to *slow down* their activity and production to stay within their comfort zone.

When you're hot, don't stop.

Keep going.

Take advantage of the momentum.

How Having NO-Goals™ Corrects the Situation

Now let's look at what would have happened if Jill had been operating with a NO-Goal rather than a success quota.

Let's assume that Jill has the capacity to make three sales calls a day, four days a week—with the fifth day spent in the office. Of her twelve sales calls, Jill's goal is to close three sales (or 25 percent).

Now what if instead of having set a YES-Goal of three, Jill had set a NO-Goal of nine? If she had (using our previous example), here's what would have happened: Monday Jill would have made three calls, and after she got her three sales, she would have said to herself: "Wow, I haven't gotten a single no yet. I'm behind!"

Rather than slow down, Jill would have had to speed up in order to reach her goal of nine noes for the week. See the difference?

- YES-Goals would have led to fewer calls (and standard production)

- NO-Goals would have led to more calls (and, most likely, greater production)

And what do you think would happen? Chances are that Jill would obliterate her goal for the week. And, if she kept it up, she'd blow her goal for the month out of the water. That's the power of setting NO-Goals!

One of the great ironies is that having too great an emphasis on success can lead to failure—while placing an emphasis on increasing your failure can lead to massive increases in your success.

Are we saying that you should ditch your YES-Goals entirely? Well, maybe. If your fixation on those goals is slowing your performance, then—by all means—yes. Shift your attention exclusively to the behaviors necessary to achieve them (in this case, the behavior of hearing no more often). Because when you focus on *going for no*, the yeses will come automatically.

They always do.

Ray Higdon's Take...

The Chicken List

One of the terms I hear a lot is "the chicken list." It's a list of people who someone may be afraid to call because the people are wealthier perhaps or more socially connected with a higher perceived level of status. The reason someone is afraid to call these people is the assumption that they'll be more likely to reject them, or that the rejection may be more harmful somehow than rejection from your friends or neighbors—which may or may not be true.

Most people, when they come into network marketing, tend to look for people who they perceive as below them socially. Perhaps they feel like maybe they have a little bit of influence over them, or maybe they think that person needs what they have.

The thing you need to understand when it comes to the chicken list is that people who have the fastest success in network marketing are typically those who are more socially connected. Also, the person who is wealthier and more socially connected usually has a more open mind.

From my personal experience, if you want to witness the most closed-minded people, go to your broke friends. The people who need what you have the most, the people who really need to make money and are struggling—usually they're the most skeptical and cynical.

I have a lot of examples of reaching out to people that, at least at the time, I thought were more socially connected than me. One of them was a gentleman named Ron Legrand. Ron is a real-estate investor and trainer based out of Jacksonville, Florida.

When I was focused on becoming the top income earner in my company, I knew that if I could get Ron onboard, I could persuade him to let me on his different speaking stages.

So, through a friend, I was able to get on the phone with him. I told him, "Hey, fit me in any corner of any of your speaking engagements. I only require twenty-five minutes, and I'll close 10 percent of the room. If you put me out there, test me out, and if you don't like it then, obviously, you can back out."

Ron signed up, and he snapped me into some different events. I never spoke for more than twenty-five minutes, and I always closed more than 10 percent of the room. I put everyone on his team, made him a little bit of money, and it worked out well. I also made some good friends through doing that. I met some great, highly connected people that way, and it was a pretty cool experience.

Now, admittedly, this isn't something most people might do. But it's a great example of how approaching people on your chicken list can impact your business.

Kai Deering

I had never been in a Networking Marketing company before. In fact, I didn't even know my company was networking until about one year later! I did however, come from a sales background so, I did know a few things that translated well in this business.

One, you are going to be bad before you are good. Anyone who has ridden a bike before knows you are going to fall down and get bloodied, but eventfully you will figure it out. That's exactly how success in this industry happens.

In the beginning, if you are like me, you are going to do it all wrong. I talked too much, violated the laws of duplication and built a team that fell apart at least once until I started to figure it out. Unfortunately, sometimes we figure out what works by figuring out what doesn't work, which is more painful than if we were just more coachable from the onset.

That being said, you can't be bad enough—even when you start out that people won't at least register, sometimes out of pity.

Which leads to the second thing I know, people aren't numbers but this is a numbers game and if you show your opportunity to enough people, a pattern will appear. It's something I call F.U.N., the Fundamental Understanding of Numbers and if you track how many people you have exposed verses the number that sign up as an agent or use your product or services you will learn a lot.

You will see improvement with the exposure to registration ratio and exactly how to crank up your activity to get the results you desire because we can't control our results, we can only control our activity.

So, I started going through the numbers, improving along the way and tracking. What I found was amazing!

During the first million-dollars I earned with the company, I exposed about 11,000 people, recruited about 300 associates and wrote about 1,300 memberships.

When I looked at the F.U.N., I realized that one in every 8.4 people I showed this to became a customer and 23% of those also became associates!

So, every associate I personally sponsored was worth $3,000 whether they did anything or not! That F.U.N. drives me in the business to continue to go through the numbers, because for every person that tells me no, I make about $100. Stay the course and success is imminent.

Now that's F.U.N.

- Kai Deering, Millionaire Club Member, Speaker, Trainer and Network Marketing Professional, www.KaiDeering.com

Increase the Noes in Each Interaction

Approaching someone and getting a yes or a no is one way to go for no. Another way is to get a no (or a number of noes) after someone has said yes.

For example, imagine someone who sells suits for a living. There is the first part of the sale—the suit itself. In other words, turning a looker into a buyer. But after a customer has said yes, that doesn't mean the sale is over. There are many numerous opportunities to hear additional noes.

For example: Another suit. a sport coat, dress slacks, shirts, ties, shoes, socks, belts, underwear, pocket squares, and more.

During some sales it might take three or four noes to get a yes on the first suit, five more noes to get to the next item, another three noes on another item—and on and on.

All in all, during a well-crafted clothing sale, a customer might say no to twenty, thirty, maybe even forty items.

Make a list of all your products and services, and it's easy to see how many noes you could get. In addition, asking someone who else they know that may be interested in the product or in the business opportunity is a great way to increase your noes. Most people, though, get one yes and that's it. They don't want to push their luck.

Yes is rarely the end of a sale, or at least it shouldn't be. In many cases, yes is just the beginning.

And remember: It takes no more energy to get a BIG NO than to get a small one. After all, no is a no is a no—no matter who it's coming from or how big the opportunity.

As the saying goes:

"Easy yeses produce little successes."

Ray Higdon's Take...

On Money Mindset

When I started in network marketing, I was dead broke. It took a while for me to stop assuming that the people I was dealing with had the same challenges, the same money restrictions. Because I was dead-broke, I had to fight my urge to think that everyone else was dead-broke too.

One of the questions that helped me get past the issue was to ask, "What kind of budget have you got to start a home-based business?" There were times when people said zero, and times when people told me $10,000. At that time, I could barely scrape together $500, so it was important not to assume that my challenges were the same as everyone else's.

I hear people say things all the time that contradict this way of thinking. I hear people say, "Well, no one's got money right now." That is never true, of course. Not ever. If you believe that, you're going to lose before you even start. You're going to lose before you even pick up the phone.

My suggestion is to understand that by accepting other's claims of poverty you're creating obstacles and excuses that really aren't there. But if you're willing to make enough contacts and hit your no-goal, you'll find plenty of people who will say yes.

You must understand that just because you limped into the company for the bare minimum ninety-dollar package because it was all you could afford, that doesn't mean there won't be plenty of people willing to start for the $1,000 package. Never assume. Ask the questions. I've met people who have limped into a company for ninety dollars, only to go to an event weeks later and say, "Wait a minute—there's a bigger package? Man, I didn't even know. I totally would have started there."

As a result, the person who needed the money the most just missed out on a nice commission had they just asked the question. But they didn't. And, in the process, they forced the other person on the same low-end plan they were on.

Never Make Decisions for Others

One of the worst things a salesperson can do is to prejudge someone's ability or willingness to buy what they have. In other words, to say no for the customer.

Your opinion about whether a person will say yes or no is exactly that—*an opinion.*

Whatever *you* think someone will decide to do, or how much you think someone has to spend, is presumptive and irrelevant. The only thing that matters is what the prospective customer thinks and is willing to spend.

Now why is it that people tend to prejudge others?

Simple.

The reason we prejudge is to eliminate the need to have them say no to us. But if your goal is increase the number of noes you hear, then prejudging makes no sense whatsoever.

Does it?

To prejudge someone because they may say no is to engage in self-rejection, where we say no to ourselves without even giving the prospect the chance.

You must give everyone the opportunity to say no to you because if you don't, you're simply saying no to yourself.

The truth is that self-rejection is the worst kind of rejection there is. If someone else rejects you, okay. It's painful sometimes, but you can live with that. Right?

But to reject yourself? That's not just painful—it's criminal.

Ray Higdon's Take...

On Prejudging

It's extremely important not to prejudge others, and I've had to learn this lesson over and over.

Never prejudge anyone.

Ever.

Some people are very adamant about wearing their success on their sleeve, dressing to the nines and looking super sharp. And I can tell you from attending hundreds of events over the years—in different countries all over the world—the sharpest, best-dressed person is often the most over-leveraged, dead-broke person in the room. And the person you're sitting next to—the one in the overalls that you've been ignoring all night—that person is a millionaire. You simply never know.

This is especially true of your cold market, of course. But it can be true of your warm market, too. A lot of people just don't talk about how much money they have to invest in a business, even people you think you know really well. You have zero idea what their real net worth is. For example, how much money do your parents have in their savings account right now? Or your next-door neighbors? Or the person who sits across from you at work?

You just can't judge.

You can also never judge how hungry someone is—meaning their internal motivation—by what you know about them or by how they look. You can't judge someone's hunger or passion until you see them in the game.

When my buddy invited me to a home meeting back in July of 2009, I was still broke, in personal foreclosure, and being chased by bill collectors. I had been in this funk for about a year. I was not clinically depressed but probably borderline depressed. Life just wasn't a bowl of cherries at the time. If asked to present my resume to someone, it wouldn't have been pretty. I wasn't in just one foreclosure—I was in eight.

All my real-estate investment properties were being whisked away. My financial shape was worse than bad. And I could easily have been prejudged.

But the one thing that doesn't show up on a resume is your hunger for success. I was hungry. I was going to make it happen, come hell or high water. I didn't know exactly how, but I was going to dig myself out of the hole that I was in—and I did.

Within five months, I was earning $10,000 a month. Month seven, I was at $40,000. Month ten, $50,000. No one could have known that based on my clothing, my resume, or my initial bank account.

You can't judge someone's level of hunger, and hunger is—in my opinion—the biggest predictor for whether someone's going to make it happen in this business. In any business.

One thing that I've learned over the years is you don't have to be broke to be hungry, or have your back against the wall to be hungry. You don't have to be any of those things to be hungry.

I've met some mega-millionaires over the years, but they are so hungry that they outwork all of their competition. They outwork every broke person they know because they're hungry. That's how they became wealthy in the first place. And even if they aren't hungry for more money, they may be hungry to grow. They may be hungry to impact more people. I can tell you right now, looking at my life, I believe I'm actually hungrier now than I was when I was broke.

So how do you know whom to approach? How can you tell who's got the hunger to succeed? You can't. The only thing you can do is the smart thing.

Never prejudge.

Ask everyone.

Never assume.

For example, we have one gentleman that joined our coaching program. He borrowed the money to take our training. I didn't know this at the time, and I hate to admit it, *but if I had known he was borrowing the money, I might have dissuaded him from joining. But he borrowed money as the deposit to join our coaching program, and two years later he did over $50,000 in one month.*

The reason I tell this story is this: What if I had prejudged him and said, "Oh, he doesn't have money. He works at a low-paying job. He's not a good prospect." I would not only have prejudged him—I would have misjudged him. And had I done that, we both would have lost out. On what planet would that have been the right thing to do?

So when it comes to prospecting, don't judge people. Just talk to them. I don't care if I'm talking to the mayor of our town or if I'm talking to a homeless person—I'm not invested in the outcome. I don't need them to join my business. I also don't need their acceptance or approval. I'm never working from a position of desperation.

My posture is that whatever they say, it just doesn't matter. You've probably heard people talk about posture before, but they never explained it to you.

Posture is your belief in what you're doing, what you represent, or what you have—without the requirement for external acceptance or approval. So when it comes to prospecting, I don't judge people, and I don't allow myself to be addicted to the outcome. This allows me to approach anyone. Because who knows? The person who is dead-broke and in foreclosure today, like I once was, may be the top income earner a few months from now. I don't know. Neither do you.

And some of the people who aren't winners right now can become winners—or can refer you to winners.

Around 2010, there was a lady I was friends with (who I'm still friends with) and she was in a tough spot financially. Her mother was very sick, but she really wanted to join the business. She just was having a tough time coming up with the money, so I teamed her up with someone and together they came up with the money. So, right away it doesn't sound like a great prospect, right?

Well, day one of her being in the business, she gets me on the phone with someone who was a former diamond in a company. I talked to him on the phone and could immediately tell he was a quality person. That guy put thousands and thousands of people on my team.

Had I judged her, I never would have met the guy. He lived all the way across the country in California. I live in Florida.

I would never have come across him, and he never would have joined my team. A woman who looked like she didn't have much chance of succeeding made the introduction, and everyone won because of it.

So, don't prejudge anyone. Ever. They may never be an all-star, but they may know a few.

Bob Quintana

When I look at my 10+ years in network marketing, it's sort of been a "Go for No!" epic drama.

I was running a successful management consulting business for many years and was doing really well. It was the typical entrepreneurial small-business model where you're making a lot of money, but you're running like crazy and I just got tired of trading time for money.

I always said if I ever left the consulting business, network marketing would be one of the things that I'd seriously consider. I finally just got to the point where I realized that my consulting business was never going to be able to create the kind of leverage I wanted.

One of my favorite 'go for no' examples is what my sponsor did to me.

I had actually called him several years earlier to try to get him into the first company I was with.

He was a very successful entrepreneur and when I showed him the business he told me, "Bob, I appreciate it. But I'm a traditional business guy. I'll never do network marketing."

About three years later I got a phone call from this same guy with "an opportunity."

You've got to be kidding me, right?

Now, I'd hit the Diamond rank about seven months earlier, but the company was going through some problems. He asked if he could stay in touch with me though, and I said, of course.

He put me on his mailing list and every week he would send a newsletter out to his whole team, and I was on that list. He'd talk about how well things were going, how they had 150 people at their weekly meeting, things like that. I admit I was looking at the emails. I was happy for him, but my business was going through difficulties.

He would call me every few weeks and he'd say, "Hey Bob, how are you doing? How's it going? Would you just take a look?" And I kept saying, "No, no, no, no, no, no."

After about five months of this, he called me on a day where, in all honesty, my business was not going great and I really didn't feel like listening to how well he was doing.

I finally told him, "I'm really happy that you're doing well. But I'm never going to join your company, ever. It's not going to happen. Do me a favor, take me off your email list, stop calling me. I'm never going to join your business." At that point, as I've now come to say, "he played me like a violin." He said, "You're that into the company you're with?" I said, "I bleed this company's colors. I'm so in."

He says, "Man, I must've missed something when you showed it to me three years ago." Of course, this is the guy who'd said, I'll never do network marketing!

He says, "Would you come up and show it to me again? I'll take a look at yours, but you've just got to promise to just take a look at what I'm doing." I agreed. So, we meet and he and his business partner sign-up in my business! Then he says, "Well, you know, you said you'd take a look at what I'm doing. You know it's only fair."

About halfway through his presentation I'm thinking, this is a better opportunity than the one I'm in.

I ended up being in that opportunity with him. And when that company shut down I'd become the top guy in his business and one of the top builders in the northeast. We both ended up going to the company we're currently with and now my group is a very big part of his entire business, and we've both made many millions of dollars in this opportunity. It all happened because this guy did not take "no" for an answer. Thankfully, for both our sake, he never let my telling him "no" stop him from getting me to see his opportunity, and that has positively changed both our lives forever!

- Bob Quintana, Top Network Marketing Leader, Trainer & #2 All-Time Income Earner in Company History

Stepping Over "The Line"

One fear people have is accidentally stepping over the line with a potential buyer. You know the line, right? That invisible, imaginary boundary that—if you were to step over—you'd run the risk of upsetting someone because you pushed too hard and didn't know when to quit.

This can be especially difficult when we've just gotten a yes, and now we're trying to expand the sale. How dare we ask for more?

To make matters worse, not only is the line invisible, but it's also in a different place for everyone. So, to play it safe, we do exactly that—*we play it safe*. As a result, most salespeople never get anywhere near the line.

If you adopt an attitude that under no circumstances are you ever going to risk accidentally upsetting someone by stepping over the line, there's no way you can ever perform to your full potential. Because the truth is:

The only way to discover "the line" is to step over it.

Sometimes the customer establishes the line. "I can't spend over $200," the customer might say. Or, "I can't afford to invest right now."

The amount someone tells you they're willing to spend is almost never the truth. Or, as sales trainer Ron Martin says, "Buyers are liars." What he means, of course, is that when someone tells you they have a budget or maximum amount they're willing to spend, nine out of ten times this is not really their budget—because if you've got something they really want or need, they will usually find the money.

Now we're not condoning aggressive, rude, or pushy behavior. But we are saying that most of us need to be more assertive and, as such, every now and then we're going to accidentally step over the line. If you never step over the line, how can you ever know if you've maximized the opportunity?

Ray Higdon's Take...

Stepping Over the Line

I do not believe it's ever a good idea to be pushy. I do, however, believe in being <u>pully</u>.

For example, you can be pully by painting a picture or creating a vision that someone wants to be a part of—that pulls them toward you, your product, your opportunity.

"Why?" is one of the most powerful questions you can ask. I have tons of examples, so let me give you one.

Let's say you're following up with someone who watched your company presentation and has told you no. You might want to ask them this question: "Hey, I'm just curious. When I originally reached out to you, you watched the company video. Do you mind if I ask you why? What were you hoping to gain? Was there something you were hoping to see that maybe you didn't?"

Getting someone into that kind of conversation will tell you a lot about the person. More importantly, it will tell you about their goals, dreams, problems, etc.

I believe in asking questions and learning about people because what they tell me about themselves is infinitely more powerful and important than delivering a sales pitch, trying to push something on them.

I may call and say, "Hey, I know you said that what we have isn't a fit for you, but I just won a cruise from my company and I'm curious if you know anyone who might want to earn a vacation if we showed them how to do it?"

Now, is that pushy? No, that's not pushy. But it is pully. They may see themselves on a cruise like that and the vision of the vacation might pull them toward learning more or giving the business a try—even though they just said no a few days earlier. Or, at a minimum, it may pull them to the point where they'll ask me some questions.

Pushy would be, "Hey, I just won a cruise. Wouldn't you like to win one? Wouldn't you like to run with me and lock arms and make this thing happen?" That is pushy. It's not overly pushy, but it is pushy.

Pully is when you're asking questions that can make them want more information—you're increasing their curiosity.

Here's another example. Let's say I go to a company event and someone crosses the stage and says, "Hey, I used to be a bus driver, and now I'm making $1 million a year." Well, I'm going to write that down, and then I'm going to find every bus driver I can and call them and say, "Hey, I know this might not be a fit for you, but I know you're a bus driver. I was just at an event, and there was another bus driver there who's making a lot of money right now. So I was wondering if you know any bus drivers who might be open to making extra money? Enough that might allow them to retire early perhaps?"

That's pully.

If they're interested, they'll be pulled toward the picture I've painted of a bus driver—just like them—who is making enough money to retire early. Maybe enough money to even make them wealthy.

Here's the thing, though. If the person isn't pulled toward the vision enough to start asking questions, I'm not going to say, "Well, what about you? Would you be interested?" To me, that would be pushy.

Pushy salespeople tend to raise resistance in others. Pully salespeople, like what we teach at my company, tend to raise the temperature. They try to increase the other person's curiosity, to see if they have someone who is hungry— someone wanting and eager for more.

Anna Khanna

I just finished university and our family business is catering. We used to go to a market on Sunday, and the store opposite us sold greetings cards and wrapping paper. The couple that ran the store always went on holiday, had new shoes, a new car, and they were very positive. We asked them what else they did and they showed me. Then I went to a presentation and I loved it straight away. I knew that it could fit around our family business. When I saw the opportunity that I could make a lot of money, and plus I've never wanted to rely on a man for money either, I thought it was perfect—the perfect opportunity.

The first three years in network marketing I was in my early 20's, and I used to go to the trainings, I would hear about everyone else—how they used to get customers and distributors, and I never used to get any.

Everyone said 'no' to me.

They'd say to me, "Well, not everyone says 'no,' – you've only had about two or three no's in a row."

Even when I used to see my auntie or my uncle they used to say "no," so I'd go home and cry to my Mom and say it was too hard and I couldn't do the business. Then I'd go back to a training and I'd go out there, but every time someone would say 'no' to me, I would not speak to anyone for weeks or sometimes a month at a time because I thought: they're going to say 'no' so there's no point in asking anyone.

My friend Chris recommended the 'Go for No' book, and said don't read the book because you haven't got time; you're always in the car so get the audio book on CD and listen to it. I listened to it every day for months and months and that helped me get to where I am in the business. I think if it wasn't for that book I probably would have quit or been in the same position I was then.

If I sit at home and I'm having an office day I'll just hit the phone, one call after another—I wouldn't have been able to do that before either. I'm constantly on the phone.

It's also to the point where I feel a good connection with someone and I know they'll be really good, it's hard not to sort of piss them off as well - but I still have never given up hope.

Then there's my friend Emma. Every time there was something new with the company, like a new announcement, or a new incentive, I'd always tell her and she'd say, "Oh, I haven't got time!"

She did say to me, and we talk about this onstage together: "I only joined to shut you up, and it was only 50 pounds to join, so I just thought it would be 50 pounds well spent just to shut you up." She nearly blocked me on Facebook, I was that annoying!

We've become very good friends now. She's been in the business for two years and now she thanks me for not giving up on her because the business has changed her life for her family.

As for me, I've achieved company cars, amazing holidays, and I am in the top 1% of the company - and one of the youngest females who has achieved my leadership position. In fact, I just got a brand-new Mercedes on the 1st of the month. It had 8 miles on the clock.

That was amazing.

- Anna Khanna, Top 1% Earner in Co. (whilst still working 60+ hrs. in the family catering business)

Every No Has Hidden Information

Every no you <u>obtain</u> holds within it valuable information needed to move forward with a prospect and/or improve performance with future prospects. And the use of the word *obtain* here is quite intentional.

Webster's defines obtain as to "gain or acquire." And that's exactly the way we see it, and so should you. You should always think of the word *no* as something you've gained or acquired. In that way, obtaining a no is better than hearing, "Let me think about it."

Allowing a sales interaction to end with the customer saying, "Let me think about it" poses three problems:

1) It often deludes us into thinking we're making progress when in reality we are not.

2) More often than not, "let me think about it" is really just a no in disguise. The truth is they're not really going to think about it—they just want to brush you off.

3) It makes it harder to discover the reason they're not saying yes because "let me think about it" puts an end to the conversation.

And, as such, we believe that getting a no is always better than having someone say they want to think about it, where days drag into weeks and weeks drag into months—without ever turning into a definitive decision. At least a no sets you up to ask, "Sure. May I ask why?"

We interviewed top performers to find out what goes through their minds when they get a no. The thoughts usually followed one of three paths:

Thought #1:
"Good. We're getting somewhere."

Top sales performers don't think, "Well, that's the end of that." They think the exact reverse.

They think, "And now we begin!"

As countless top performers have told us, "The sale doesn't start until after the first no. Everything before that is simply getting to the starting line."

Thought #2:

"What does this no really mean?"

Top performers go into consultant mode and continue the information gathering process. They know that behind every no there is usually a treasure trove of hidden information—information that, if able to be uncovered, can be of amazing value.

Thought #3:

"Where did I go wrong? What did I miss?"

Finally, when top sales performers hear no, they never get mad or blame the customer. Instead, they wonder if there was anywhere in the process they could have done a better job of presenting the offer, answering the prospect's questions, and/or addressing their concerns. In other words, *they get curious.*

And they're not pretending to be curious just to stay in the sale—*they're really curious*—because they know that behind every no is the information they need to get to yes. And even if they *don't* get to yes, top performers want to learn the reason(s) for the no because the information may be helpful with another customer somewhere down the road.

The truth is most sales end without ever knowing the reason for the no. The result, of course, is that we often end up repeating many of the same errors and mistakes over and over again, sometimes for an entire career.

Ray Higdon's Take...

Dealing with "I'm Not Interested"

Dealing with people who say they're not interested is an interesting situation. I'm a big fan of energy management. If someone is energetically backing away from the sale by saying, "No, I'm not interested," the typical response is to press harder—which is the exact opposite of what I find most beneficial.

When most people are told by someone they're not interested, they press with, "Well, why not? This thing's awesome, man! Come on. Don't you want to get rich?" The untrained individual tends to mismanage energy, and so this is why rejection happens. This is why rejection saps more energy from untrained people than it does from someone who is properly trained.

When I was actively building a network marketing business, people would often tell me, "No, I'm not interested. Not my kind of thing."

When someone says no to my offer, I'm not going to say anything that is even remotely hostile or passive aggressive— like: "Why not, man? You know this is really cool and you'd do great!" There's zero of that—none—not one iota of it. But I do plant a persuasive phrase in their head by saying, "Hey, do you know anyone that would want to make some extra money if we showed them step-by-step how to do it?"

In this way, the focus isn't on them anymore. Although, when I say that, about 50 percent of the time the person will reevaluate their decision. They'll usually say something like, "Well, wait a minute. You guys have a plan? You have a step-by-step way you teach people how to do this and make money?" Now all of the sudden we're back in the conversation about them possibly joining or buying without me really trying. Other times, the person will respond with, "You know what, I do know somebody. Here's a referral."

Anytime you can get a referral from someone who told you no, that's powerful because you're leveraging your time.

NO doesn't mean never.
NO means not yet.

Woody Allen said that 80 percent of success is simply showing up. The part he left out is that you don't just have to show up—you have to *keep* showing up! In other words, you have to demonstrate persistence.

Is this to suggest that when attempting to sell someone you should keep showing up forever?

No.

Winston Churchill is famous for having said, "Never, never, never quit!" In reality, it's important to know when to stop showing up. The problem is that most people think the time to quit has come long before it actually has.

The answer to success usually lies somewhere between Woody and Winston.

One Size Does Not Fit All

So, how many times do you need to hear NO to know you've heard enough? Unfortunately, one size does not fit all.

But to get you started, consider the following selling statistics:

- 44 percent of sales people give up after hearing one no.

- 22 percent more give up after hearing a second no.

- 14 percent more give up after hearing a third no.

- 12 percent more give up after hearing a fourth no.

This means that 92 percent of all salespeople give up after obtaining only four noes from a prospect. Yet the same research project determined that 60 percent of all customers say no *four times* before they finally say yes!

Well, it doesn't take a rocket scientist to tell us the minimum number of times you should call a qualified prospect is five—always done in positively persistent, non-aggressive ways.

Ray Higdon's Take...

Dealing with Negative People

If someone is rude to me, I understand they may be struggling in their life. And I may feel bad for them, so I'll just tell them, "You know what, I understand. I understand how you feel. I'm sorry that whatever's going on in your life you feel you need to say that, but I wish you the best." Then I hang up and move on.

However, what's interesting is that somewhere from 30 percent to 40 percent of people will immediately apologize. So while I will not call them back, sometimes they will call me back. And if someone calls me back and apologizes, then okay. I'm an easy forgiver.

But let me say this: I've encountered some very nasty people over the years. I've had people say some very disgusting things to me and about me—even about my family. So if someone curses me out or says something overly negative, I no longer want that person around me. They cannot join my team. That's the deal. Period. They've disqualified themselves and get completely etched off the list because I value my lifestyle more than money.

When I was actively building my business, people would ask, "What customer relationship management tool do you use?" Me? I used a yellow pad and my phone. I would schedule things in my iPhone calendar and make notes on a yellow legal pad. And most of the time I didn't even take much in the way of notes, but that's just how I did it. That doesn't mean it's the only way. It doesn't mean it's the perfect way.

Assuming someone said no, and they weren't overly rude or super nasty, I would put a little check by their name letting me know I'd reached out to them. Each check mark would let me know how many times they'd said no.

When I'd call them back, I'd immediately address the elephant in the room by saying, "Listen, a few months ago I reached out to you about this thing. I know you said no and that it's not a fit for you, but it's really blowing up. In fact, we've got

*one substitute teacher in Orlando that just made $10,000."
Then I'll share a story that explains why I'm calling them. By
the way, the best method to generate stories like that is to
attend your company events and pay close attention to the
rewards and recognition portion of the event. You always
hear some deep, rich, powerful story you can use as a way to
contact a prospect again.*

*If I share a story I heard about someone going from sleeping
on mom's couch to making $100,000 a year, how could
anyone argue with that? That's a real story. It really
happened, so pay attention to those stories.*

*If you're not sure how to start the conversation, just use
something like this: "We just had a (insert story here), and I
wanted to reach out to you to see if you know any
(_____) that might be looking for extra money. We can
show them step-by-step how to do it."*

*Now that's a deflection question. Many times, the person will
say, "Well, wait a minute. Tell me a little bit more about this."
And then—to save face—they may say something like, "You
know when you originally reached out to me it was bad
timing, but now I'm thinking it's a little better."*

*Well, it wasn't really usually bad timing—the truth is <u>you</u> just
came with a better story.*

*Make no mistake: There are deep riches in the list of people
who have told you no. Keep track of them. Unless someone is
really, really rude, I don't ever mark him or her off my
follow-up list.*

Paula Pritchard

I was teaching at Kent State University and finishing up the last part of my PhD. One of my professors said, Paula, how would you like to make some money during the summer? I was ambitious and said, absolutely! That was the first time I had ever been introduced to a network marketing business. I sat in the living room of a colleague, I saw them draw some circles and decided I'd give it a try.

For the next 15-months I struggled and experienced the ups and downs that go with that learning curve. 15 months into it, I made the decision to go full speed and really commit to it. Once I made that commitment, it all started to come together for me.

But one of the things that you hear a lot and I took it to heart, was that the people on the stage heard more no's. I figured that's why it paid so well. And that's why everyone on the stage welcomed them with open arms and we gave them such accolades, because we know the pain, the disappointment, the discouragement that they went through and they still did it anyway. Once I understood that - I knew it was something I couldn't avoid. I was going to have to go through that.

So, what I did was I would put on a "psychological armor" and I would envision that no one could penetrate the armor - not bullets, not arrows, and not no's. I would also try to lessen my emotions. I tried to level my emotions and keep myself emotionally detached. When I would talk to someone, it didn't matter whether they said yes or no because I was emotionally detached. I had on my armor. I got to the point where I'd rather have a no than a yes.

I started to understand that noes and yesses were actually equal, and it was more of a numbers game. I started to go through the numbers. I made calls day-in and day-out - irrelevant if it was raining, if it was snowing, if I had the flu, I still made the calls. I committed to myself how many I would make and making the call was my success.

Despite all the different fears I had initially, just making the call was a success. It didn't matter whether they answered, it didn't matter whether they were home, whether they said yes or if they said no. I was already successful because I actually picked up the phone and dialed. When I made that my point of success, I was successful a lot during the day!

There's no shortcuts. We all have to go through it, but understand when you come out the other side you're glad you did it because you're different, and you're better, and you're stronger, and you just feel so good about yourself because you did it.

So, after three or four years I went totally fulltime in network marketing and never looked back. And that's been over 30 years ago!

- Paula Pritchard, Top Network Marketing Earner, Trainer, and Author of www.owningyourself.com.

To Qualify or To Disqualify:
That Is the Question!

Determining if someone is a qualified buyer—or if they should be *disqualified* as a prospect for your product, service, idea, or opportunity—has two critical elements:

- *The first is want.*
- *The second is need.*

Our position is simple: you should never disqualify someone because they *don't yet want* what you have to offer, but you should disqualify everyone for whom *no need* exists.

Selling is, at its core, the art and science of creating want (or generating desire, if you will). So, if you think about it, to disqualify someone because they've yet to agree to meet with you is to disqualify them because *you* have not yet done your job. Imagine actually saying to someone, *"I've determined that you are not qualified to buy my product or service because I have yet to successfully convince you to consider what I've got—even though you need it!"*

Need is an entirely different animal, however.

To invest time pursuing someone who has no need for what you've got is an insane waste of time. It is also the epitome of what people abhor about salespeople—the selfish desire to force something on someone when there is no need for it.

The *lack of need*, therefore, is an immediate disqualifier for the honest salesperson. Conversely, the *presence of need* is an automatic qualifier. It's that simple.

How long should you keep approaching a truly qualified prospect? Our answer is: *for as long as it takes.*

Ray Higdon's Take...

Success Rate

There are two main options for building a business. The one most talked about in network marketing is prospecting. The other one is marketing.

Prospecting is active. You're reaching out to potential customers and having one-on-one conversations. It can be online or offline, and cold market or warm market. It's you reaching out to an individual.

When it comes to prospecting, always work to increase your closing ratio. That means working on your skills, how you phrase things, and different ways to handle objections. Those skills are always good to develop.

Marketing, on the other hand, is passive. You're doing something that you hope will connect with an unnamed, unseen individual. It could be an advertisement, a video, a flyer, a blog post, banner ad, a craigslist ad—there are lots of different ways.

Most network marketing companies—as well as most network marketing up-lines—teach prospecting. They don't teach marketing, though. Hardly anyone teaches marketing.

In marketing, you craft messages that attract people to you, and that allows you to have a higher close ratio than prospecting. Of course, that doesn't mean you should stop reaching out to those you don't think you can convert.

The biggest lesson for me is this: When I reach out to a prospect, my first reaction isn't to close them but to see if they'll listen. That's it. Are they open? And what that does for you energetically—when that's your focus instead of "I really want to close this person"—makes a big difference in how you come across to the prospect. You're more genuine than if you talked about your deal, opportunity, or business. You don't come across pushy, needy, or desperate.

But most importantly— and I think one of the core concepts of Go for No!—is that you're not energetically destroyed if they don't join your deal. Whereas, if you're talking to people and your main goal is to get a sale today, then you may be more invested than you should be. And that's typically not a good thing.

I've been blessed to have some of the top closers on my network marketing teams over the years. I've even had multiple people personally recruit over five hundred people. Whether due to their savvy skill set or perhaps their marketing, they can often close over 30 percent.

Sound far-fetched? You can close that many people, too. You can beat the best closers by talking to more people. If the super-closer talks to ten people and gets three—well, you can talk to one hundred people and get ten, and you win. People beat themselves up way too much over closing percentages. They think they need to close everybody, and nobody can do that.

If your goal is to blow it up and "crush it" in your business, then who really cares whether you have a low closing percentage? Just go talk to more people—that's how you're going to get more people involved in your business.

Jessica Higdon

I had a girl in our office that had tried to introduce me to a company and I thought it looked great. I came home from college and I showed my parents. My dad is a very successful entrepreneur and he looked at it and said, "Pyramid scheme. Scam." So. I kind of dismissed it and thought, "Well if he thinks that's what it is, then that's what it must be."

The business that I ended up building really appealed to me mainly because the product was something a little different than I had seen before. I jumped in not knowing really anything about business, not knowing anything about network marketing at all, just knowing that I liked the model. I was also going against all my family members so, obviously, none of them joined.

I was 21 years old and no warm-market whatsoever, so the first six months I didn't sign-up a single person, not one. I felt like I was working really hard and working super long hours, and not getting anywhere. I was only trained to go to my warm-market, which is good, but then from there sometimes we need a "now what?"

So, after six months of not signing up a single person, I went on Google and thought, "How can I build this online?" I found some people that had built businesses on social media, both networking businesses and traditional businesses and it gave me hope.

When you prospect face-to-face you're definitely going to see rejection for sure. When you do it on social media, because they're so "cold" you really have to warm them up, so you hear "no" a majority of the time. I was reaching out to 20 to 30 people a day and most days I would hear "no, not even willing to look at it" from at least 17 or 18 of those 20.

What I learned on social media is it's all about numbers and learning how to turn those people that are "no's" right now into warmer contacts that you can convert later because on social media people are always watching you. So, I never really took them as a "no" but I did hear it on a daily basis, and a lot of those people did come back to me later.

At first it was really hard. I felt like I wanted to quit pretty much on a weekly basis. Then once I got my first sign-up, I thought if this works once, it can work again. Then you get your second sign-up and you get a little more confidence, and then you get your third, and your fourth, and your fifth, and on and on. All of a sudden it becomes easier, and then you get your first leader who actually goes out and starts creating that duplication that we all hear about.

That really starts to build your confidence and you realize OK, yes, I can do this. My advice to all of my team members when we were building was, "Hey, if you don't want to quit pretty consistently in the beginning then you're just not working hard enough, because if it were easy, everybody would do it."

I also always tell people 0 to $1,000 is so much harder than $1,000 to $10,000 in income because you're figuring out the system - what works and what doesn't. You're figuring out yourself too and how to get that confidence. So, you'll go through some trial and error and you'll go through a lot of "no's," but at the end of the day whether it's face-to-face, or social media, or whatever, it's about the numbers and it's about how much time you allow yourself.

From not signing up a single person for six months, with a lot of trial and error through prospecting on social media, I was finally able to have my first $10,000 month after 18 months. From there I became the #1 female income earner in that company. I was so successful in figuring out a system, I have now trained thousands of others to do what I did!

- Jessica Higdon, Speaker, Best Selling Author &
Top Social Media Recruiting Trainer

Why People Quit Network Marketing

Let's be clear: That people "quit" network marketing is not the problem. The fact that they quit is the *result*—in other words, the *consequence* of the problem. What needs to be addressed is the *cause* of people quitting. The *reason* they quit.

The problem—or problems since there are two—is as follows:

Problem #1:

The fear of failure and rejection

Problem #2:

How leaders deal with it (or, more accurately, don't deal with it)

Ultimately, this is every person's biggest roadblock to growth—*and ultimate threat to survival.*

How big a problem is it? We surveyed over four hundred business professionals about their fears and motivations. First we asked:

What is the biggest fear on the part of a salesperson?

- 51 percent said that the customer would say no and reject them.

- 22 percent said upsetting people by coming across pushy or aggressive.

- 18 percent said <u>not</u> making the sale or reaching their sales goal.

- Only 9 percent said they were concerned that the product was right for the customer!

Next, we asked:

What is the #1 quality of a great salesperson?

- 38 percent said the willingness to face rejection.

- 22 percent said ability to close the sale.

- 18 percent said communication and negotiation skills.

- Only 5 percent said product knowledge!

Finally, we asked:

When it comes to dealing with rejection in sales, which is most difficult?

- 27 percent said making the initial contact call.

- 37 percent said following-up with someone who had already said no at least once.

Let it suffice to say the fear of failure and rejection costs the network marketing industry millions, if not billions of dollars.

It's easy to simply dismiss people's attitudes regarding failure and rejection as something they should be able to deal with. Adults should be able to handle hearing the word *NO*, right? But in reality, the older people get, the more they tend to run from opportunities that might cause even the possibility of failure and rejection.

When we were toddlers, we took enormous risks on an hourly basis as we transitioned from crawling to walking. Even though we fell countless times, over and over again, we learned to put one foot in front of the next.

Then, as we grew older, we learned to ride our bikes through a series of failure and adjustment. Even in high school, most of us were quick to try out for a sports team or school play, knowing we could fail. Failure was simply a part of life that we never saw as final.

But then something happens. The older we get, the more we begin to fear failure and rejection. You'd think it would be the other way around, but it's not.

The problem is we start to deal with emotional failure.

For most people, failure is emotionally embarrassing, humiliating, causing people to question their aptitude and self-worth. They begin to shrink from risk, forgetting that failure is our greatest teacher. Some people equate emotional failure and rejection to physical death.

Here are some actual quotes from people on Internet chat rooms about their feelings of failure and rejection:

- *"Fear of failure and rejection are my biggest enemies."*

- *"Fear holds me prisoner."*

- *"Without fear in my life, I know I could use all the gifts given to me."*

- *"I fear moving forward, and I fear standing still."*

- *"I don't ever want to feel the pain of failure or rejection again."*

- *"I don't want to get excited by something and make an effort only to be criticized and put down."*

- *"I'd rather be dead than have to fail at anything."*

- *"I rather not try at all. While I won't succeed at anything, at least I won't fail."*

Statistically, there are not enough fearless people in the world (estimated to be less than 10 percent of the population) from which one can build an organization. As such:

> **You can't recruit exclusively from the pool of the fearless—there are simply not enough of them. The "fearful" must be recruited, too, and they must then be reprogrammed to overcome their resistance to hearing NO until they can get results and achieve success.**

One could make the case that this is their problem, not yours. Which might be true if network marketing was not a team sport.

If you are building a team:

- *Their* weakness is *your* weakness.

- *Their* decision to quit is *your* erosion.

- *Their* missed sales are *your* missed sales.

- *Their* team-building success is *your* team-building success.

- *Their* missed bonus is *your* missed future dreams.

Because like it or not:

You <u>are</u> your people.

Your people <u>are</u> you.

Ray Higdon's Take...

Why People Quit Network Marketing

Why do people quit network marketing? Well, there are a few reasons. Not necessarily in order:

They weren't properly prepared for rejection.

People quit because they don't understand that rejection is part of the process. If you're going to be in network marketing, it's not if you will get rejected—it's how much, how soon, and how often. Rejection is as natural to the process as waking up and getting dressed in the morning. If you're going to be part of this profession, you must learn to deal with rejection. If not, quitting is inevitable.

They don't remember why they started.

People often have big goals and aspirations when they join a network marketing business. They want to change this, or they want to change that. They want to fire their boss, they want to help their spouse retire early, or they want to help kids in Kenya. There are all these different reasons that drive their decision to start—and then they simply forget those reasons. Remembering why you started is very important.

They forget to consider the alternative.

Think about the alternative to you creating success. It's probably you staying right where you are. A lot of times people quit and forget to think about the ramifications of quitting. Quitting is a habit—a dangerous habit that serves as an example to your kids and others watching you. People don't usually like that one, but it's true.

They lack vision.

Another key reason people quit is because they don't know who they want to become. They don't have a vision for what they want their life to look like. They haven't invested the time to create a compelling vision for their life.

Todd Falcone

I got a phone call from some guy out of the blue and he said, "My name's Jim, I'm calling you from Orange County Marketing Group. We're a marketing company, we're looking for people that can train and manage others in the expansion of our company, we want to talk to you." That was the exact script, word-for-word. I thought I was getting recruited into a job and went down to Irvine, California.

They invited us into this presentation room, and I saw network marketing for the first time. I didn't know what a business opportunity meeting was, and watched this presentation which showed me the opportunity for $10,000 a month and no boss and thinking, "$10,000 and no boss versus the grumpy person that interviewed me at the rental car company for $1,800 a month"... and I was in.

I spent the first couple years and really didn't make any money. I made a little bit, but I was definitely behind. I ended up moving home after two years to live in my parent's house. And it is hard to get a date when you're living in your parent's house in the bunk beds as your younger brothers are off to college.

I can't tell you how many people I've sponsored because I didn't give up on them or myself. The phrase that we all hear if we're in the business for more than a week is, "the fortune is in the follow-up" and it really is. If you don't go get it, it's never going to come to you.

You may have an easy sale or sign-up every now and then, but you're not going to build a career on people that join on that first meeting. You've got to 'go for no' and you've got to keep going after somebody until they give you a flat out no, I'm not interested, leave me alone.

I remember one time I got on the phone with a guy with a lot of potential but who basically wasn't ready. I could have blown it off, and just skipped along, and forgot about him. But, three or four weeks later I called him again and he still wasn't ready.

Three or four weeks later again, I called him and he still wasn't ready.

Six months of me following up with this guy every four weeks, finally on about the sixth phone call, six months in, he says, "You are probably one of the best people that I've ever met on follow-up. You're not calling me every single day and bugging me, you're spacing it out perfectly. Guess what, I'm ready to go." And over the next 90 days he brought over 150 people into the organization. Had I blown it off, I would have never sponsored that guy.

Even though the first couple years were not a success for me financially, I got a lot of powerful education early on. If I had to go back and do it all over again, including sleeping in bunk beds and basically making no money for the first two years to get where I am now, I would do it 100 times over.

- Todd Falcone, The Fearless Networker® Network Marketing Speaker, Coach and Author

Fear is not easily measurable, which makes it easy to ignore.

The impact that fear of failure and rejection can have on your team should not be ignored. Should you decide to ignore it, you do so at your own peril—*and at significant expense.*

Yet the training around this issue—and the tools provided in most starter kits—is minimal at best.

Why?

Because fear is hard to measure.

Great performers love to track results. And there are many measurable numbers associated with turnover or churn or attrition—or whatever word you use to describe people dropping out around you.

But when you dig deeper, what you find are significant root factors that cannot be easily quantified or directly measured. Things like fear, frustration, and broken spirits that render a once-vibrant and enthusiastic team member helpless and unwilling to continue. The only way you can measure the fallout from the fear of failure, rejection, and hearing the word *NO* is after the fact. By then, of course, it's too late.

They're gone.

Part of the problem is what happens when a new team member's expectations do not match reality.

Expectation:
Everyone will be excited to join the company.

Reality:
The majority will not.

After all, they just saw the opportunity and understood the power of it—*so why wouldn't everyone join?* It's easy to see why people would think things are going to be smooth sailing.

But we know that's not the case—there will be rejection. There will be failure. There will be a lot of noes.

That's reality.

And like we just said, whenever expectations do not match reality, the result is dissatisfaction, disillusionment and the feeling that we—or the product or the opportunity—are somehow defective.

The key to solving this problem—or at least minimizing its impact—is timely inoculation.

After conducting hundreds of interviews with top up-line performers from a wide variety of network marketing companies, we've discovered inoculating people against the "failure flu" must be done BEFORE someone catches it. Because once someone's got the flu, it's too late.

That's what we believe a book like this can do: it can help set expectations and give people tools to keep their confidence up and get them inoculated to the failure flu.

Ray Higdon's Take...

Vision vs. Your "Why?"

One thing that we're attempting to do in the network marketing space is raise more awareness about what really has someone take action.

Besides consistently getting twenty noes a day, we've published over 5,000 blog posts in the last six years. We've done eight hundred podcasts. And three hundred periscopes. We do a lot, we do it consistently, and we do it every day. I'm a consistent beast. That's what people call me—a machine, a beast.

For years, people would ask, "Hey, you're so consistent. Can you teach a daily routine? Can you teach consistency?"

And so I did. The audience would ask for it, and I said, "Sure, let's do it." I would show them what I do each day. I would teach all the little steps from meditation to self-improvement to affirmations to exercises.

After analyzing the results, I noticed no one was doing it.

If you're a trainer who simply wants to get paying students and make money, you may not do this type of analysis. But I want people to adhere to what I'm teaching. I want people to change their habits and their routines. I want people to actually do something with the information.

The question I found myself asking was: What really made me so driven to do what I've done on such a consistent basis? What really led me to that level of activity for that long? And what is it that continues to drive me now?

The answer came down to a single word: vision. The vision of how I saw myself—the vision of who I wanted to become. This is not the type of thing most trainers teach. Most trainers focus on a person's "why"—you've got to have a why that is so strong it makes you cry. You've got to have a why that is bigger than you.

Don't get me wrong. Focusing on your why is great. But the issues we uncovered when it comes to your why are:

- *They're almost always external. It's about doing something <u>for</u> someone else or something external of you, and...*

- *They're very commercially digestible. For example, if I say to my friend, "You know, I'm doing this business because I want my spouse to be able to retire and spend more time with my kids," it's very easy for others to understand. No one says, "Oh, that's stupid." So, in a way, you get a payoff from sharing your why with others because it's easy for them to understand. That's what I mean by easily digestible.*

But another problem I've seen is people who have had the same "why" for ten years. They've wanted to accomplish this or that yet nothing's changed! Their level of activity hasn't changed. Their results haven't changed because habits dictate results. So rather than focus on why someone wants to do something, ask yourself this: <u>Who</u> do you want to become?

Who do you want to be? And what does that look like? How do you want others to describe you? How do you want to represent yourself as a member of your family? Who do you want to be to your descendants, to your ancestors? Who do you really want to be in this world? That involves a deeper thought and behavior change process than, "I want to retire."

<u>Who</u> rather than why.

One of my early mentors is Michael Bernard Beckwith, and Beckwith has a great quote that I share all the time:

"Pain pushes you until a vision pulls you."

I really didn't have a choice to get my twenty noes a day. That was not an option because my vision was pulling me toward it. My vision was forcing me to do it. Just like every morning when I wake up, my vision continues to pull me to deliver value to the marketplace, to put training and content out there to help other people. For me, this is non-negotiable— because of the vision I've created for myself.

I don't have to psyche myself up to create another video or do another periscope or anything like that—my vision dictates it. My vision is ruthless. It's like a supervisor or boss who tells me, "Hey, get your lazy butt up and do the things that are going to make an impact in your profession and help you fulfill who you want to become."

If we want to become the type of people who free hundreds of thousands, if not millions, of people while we're alive on this planet—if we want to become that and we're serious about it—then we have to take massive action. It's not a choice.

That is the difference. It isn't a daily routine that makes you consistent.

If we're creating a marketing course, a recruiting course— whatever it is that we're attempting to do—we almost always talk about it in terms of how it fits with our vision. Because everyone comes to the table looking for "how?" How do I do this? How do I do that? How do I approach strangers? How do I blog? How do I brand myself online? But all the questions in the world make zero difference if you don't know who you want to become. If you don't know that, then you're just not going to do it. And if you're not going to do it, then what are we doing here?

The reason most people don't get outer results is because they haven't done the inner work. They haven't determined who they want to become and what their vision is for their life.

Vision is seeing the things that you want to manifest in your life before they're there. Seeing yourself in your mind's eye as the person you truly want to become.

To be clear: My routines are not the boss of me. My vision is the boss of me.

That's what most people lack. A vision for their life. Perhaps any vison at all.

You can always spot a person with a strong vision of who they want to become because they don't need you to tell them what to do or urge them on. They do it on their own. Their vision sees to it.

Final Words...

Starting today, by applying the ideas and strategies in this book, you can eliminate any fear of failure and rejection you may still be harboring. In fact, if you're willing to work on it, you can turn no into one of the most empowering words in your life.

Because contrary to what you've heard, opportunity does not knock. You knock—*and opportunity answers*. Unfortunately, after it answers, it often says no.

The late, great boxing champion Floyd Patterson was said to have been knocked down more than any other notable fighter. "But I also got up the most," Patterson was quoted as saying. He also said, "I learned very little about myself when I won a fight. But I learned a tremendous amount about myself every time I lost."

We believe this to be true for most people. Most of us learn very little about ourselves from our successes because winning doesn't develop character.

Sales are measured by the number of times you hear yes.

Character is measured by the number of times you hear no.

We believe with all our hearts that, in the final analysis, it won't be about what you made that will matter most. It will be about what you became. Of course, if you happen to be someone who is fighting the idea of failing more, we fully understand—we all have the tendency to fight change.

Interestingly, the origin of the word *change* is from the old English cambium, which means:

"To Become."

What matters most in life is that we grow in some way, every single day—*to move toward our potential.* To get up every day and come to the edge of our abilities. To learn a little bit more. To see if we can be just a little bit better.

People who do that have a greater sense of happiness and contentment, while people who have stopped growing feel a sense of stagnation because that's exactly what they've done.

There's a saying that says, "If you want to achieve something you've never done before, you have to become someone you've never been before."

Now, if for whatever reason you still can't bring yourself to accept failure as being a good thing, then just start thinking of it as fertilizer—something that stinks but enhances growth nonetheless.

Increasing your failure rate to increase your success is one of the great truths of life—and perhaps the greatest success strategy in the world. But the magic of any strategy, no matter how powerful, is not in the knowing but *in the doing.*

Margie Aliprandi

When I first started, I was a single mom with children that were five, four, and two years of age. I didn't have any capital and I had no previous experience. Any one of those things would be a reason for somebody to say I don't want to do it or I can't do it, but instead I used my children as my reason, and I just jumped in.

But because of the lack of funds, I was unable to do some of the things I wanted to do in terms of travel. So, if somebody invited me to Louisville, Kentucky, or to Los Angeles to do a meeting, I would jump in my car, drive, sleep in my car - I did whatever it took. I also was willing to go anywhere, do meetings anywhere, and sometimes I'd drive 2-3 hours and nobody would show up.

One particular night—after I'd been working tirelessly, meetings night after night, sometimes with no one coming; sometimes maybe two people showed up; sometimes they join, and sometimes they don't—I was at the point of exhaustion, but continuing to plug along. I was headed out to a meeting, and I'd said goodbye to my kids; they're with the babysitter. As I was pulling the car around the house, my little boy - three years old at the time - comes running outside in his soccer pajamas with bare feet crying, "Mommy, don't go, don't go!" So, I pulled the car to the side of the road and got out, and what he couldn't see was that I was crying too. I didn't want to go as badly as he didn't want me to go.

I went over to him, and picked him up, and held him and I said, "Sweetheart, if you'll go inside and be a big boy, someday I'll take you everywhere I go."

As business started to develop, I had the kind of money I needed to travel. I was invited to do a meeting in New York City, and I now could afford to fly and I could stay at hotels, but I arrived late to this meeting because my cab driver could not find it.

As I came in, I could feel the irritation. I could see there was no retrieving this crowd. People were beside themselves and so I gave a very brief overview. At the end of the meeting, a Russian gentleman came up to me and he said, "I'm going to take this to Russia!"

I had quit listening to what people said. I didn't get excited by their assertions of greatness anymore; I waited to see what they were going to do. But within a handful of weeks I started noticing these names—Svetlana, Igor, Vladimir—showing up on my printout. There were pages and pages of names. Back then the printout was on single-spaced, accordion green and white paper and had 50 names on each side and stood almost a foot high. A half-million.

It was my lesson that there is a sowing season, and there is a reaping season and they are not in the same season. You've got to be willing to plant without looking at the results, or counting today's revenue, because someday you'll do meetings where no one comes, and then one day you do one meeting and you get a nation.

The end of the story with my son is, true to my word, within a couple of years I was able to take my kids all over the world.

- Margie Aliprandi Top Network Marketing Professional, Author of How to Get Absolutely Anything You Want & Co-Author, Best Worst First.

"Final, Final Thought"

There's something extra-special about people who read a book all the way to the final words. So, with that in mind, we offer this one last story. Maybe you've heard it before, maybe not.

Even if you have, we believe that sharing it now—after the important ideas we've talked about in this book—will have even greater significance. It's called:

"The Burden"

Two monks were returning to the monastery in the evening. It had rained, and there were puddles of water on the roadsides. At one place a beautiful young woman was standing, unable to walk across because of a puddle of water. The elder of the two monks went to her, lifted her up, and carried her to the other side of the road, then continued to the monastery.

In the evening, the younger monk went to the elder monk and pointed out that, as monks, they were not allowed to touch women.

"Yes, brother, this is true," the elder monk said

The younger monk replied:
"But you lifted the woman on the roadside."

The elder monk smiled and said, "Yes, I did. The difference, brother, is that I left her on the other side of the road, but apparently, you are still carrying her."

The fear of failure and rejection is a burden you don't need to carry. You can set it down and leave it behind. Right now, if you want—*or not*. Or you can carry it forever.

But, why would you?

All the best...

Richard Fenton, Andrea Waltz
and Ray Higdon

About the Authors...

Richard Fenton and Andrea Waltz

are the founders of Courage Crafters Inc. and authors of the best-selling book, 'Go for No!' along with several other business fables including their newest, 'Go for No! for Network Marketing.' Speaking on stage together, Richard and Andrea teach people in a wide variety of businesses and industries how to reprogram the way they think about the word NO, and to fail their way to success.

Their articles have been published in hundreds of online and offline journals, including several times in Success Magazine. They've written several books but 'Go for No!' is still the most popular with over 300,000 copies sold. It hit #1 on Amazon's 'Sales & Selling' Best Seller list and has remained in the top 20 for the last several years.

Richard & Andrea share daily NO-tivation on facebook (www.facebook.com/GoforNo) and on twitter (@GoforNo).

For more on Go for No!® visit: www.GoforNo.com

Ray Higdon

is a two-time bestselling author and a former #1 income earner in a network marketing company that he joined while he was in foreclosure. He has shared the stage with Tony Robbins, Bob Proctor, Les Brown, Robert Kiyosaki and many more. Ray and his wife no longer build a network marketing company so they can better serve the profession as coaches, speakers and trainers. Their coaching company was recognized on the Inc. 5,000 as one of America's fastest growing companies and they LOVE helping network marketers grow large teams and create freedom in their life. Ray blogs almost daily on www.RayHigdon.com and is the co-owner of the Higdon Group.

If you want to learn how to recruit on Social Media, Register for our next training at http://RayHigdon.com/jess

If you want to learn how to better recruit cold market prospects, Register here http://rayhigdon.com/coldmarket

If you want to learn how to implement online marketing to grow your network marketing team, register here http://rayhigdon.com/blogging

The #1 best-selling book that started it all!

A short but powerful fable, *Go for No!®* teaches the fundamentals of the GFN philosophy and the core strategies in an entertaining way you will never forget.

Yes *is* the destination, but NO is how you get there!

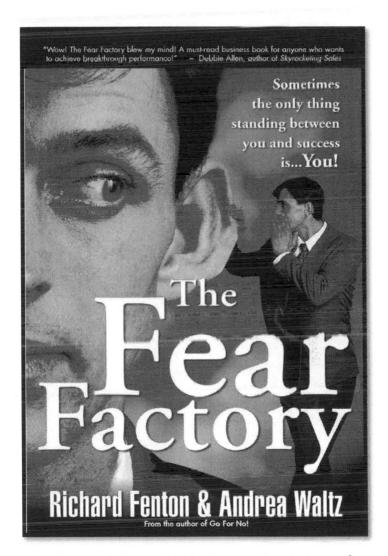

The ideal follow up book after reading *Go for No!*®

A motivational fable for anyone who struggles with fear and wants the courage to move beyond their own limitations. Sometimes the only thing standing between you and success is... YOU!

Million Dollar Year

How Much Could You Achieve in the Next 365 Days If You Really Had To?

Inspired by People and Events on Art & Ann Jonak and Tom 'Big Al' Schreiter's Annual MLM Cruise

Richard Fenton & Andrea Waltz

Authors of the #1 Amazon Sales & Selling best-seller
Go for No!® with over 200,000 copies in print!

How much could you achieve in the next 365 days if you really had to? Million Dollar Year is the story of a man who must do exactly that—someone who is finally ready to learn the lessons of network marketing from some of the best in the world. Inspired by the people and events on the annual "MLM Cruise."

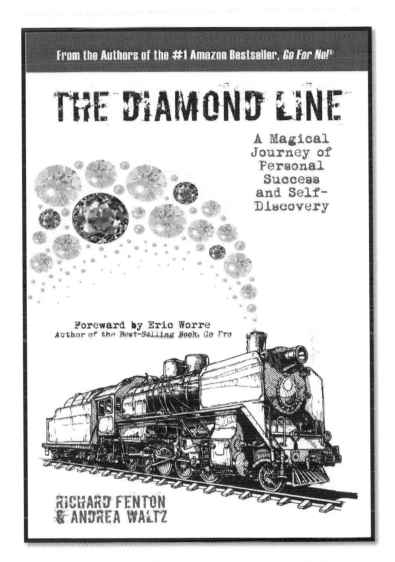

A Magical Journey of Personal Success and Self-Discovery.

A clever re-imagining of the motivational classic, Acres of Diamonds this story will transport you onto a train ride in the 1800's with some of the early masters in personal development (Foreword by Eric Worre).

RAY HIGDON'S "SIX CRITICAL CONCEPTS" for NETWORK MARKETING SUCCESS...

1. Embrace the fact that Network Marketing is a long-term endeavor, not a short-term solution. Don't expect miracles quickly and keep going.

2. The ONLY way to become a top earner is to get eyeballs on your presentation. There is no way to cut this part out.

3. For you to keep going you must have a vision for who you want to become. If you struggle with consistency, work on your vision, it will help!

4. Always understand the alternative. What happens in your life if you don't create success? Doing this can get you moving when you may not feel like it.

5. Everyone has mentors. You don't have to know it all but you should be willing to be a lifelong student.

6. You cannot reach the top without helping others. The best thing you can do for this planet is become as successful as possible because you are going to impact a lot of people in the process!

PUTTING THE GO FOR NO!®
CONCEPTS IN THIS BOOK
INTO ACTION:

1...

Create your definition of failure.

The definition we use is: *"Failure is an undeniable sign of progress toward a goal."*

We say this because, to our mind, anyone who is actively pursuing a goal or dream is NEVER a "failure"—they are merely successes in progress.

Without a positive, empowering definition of failure, failure will always be thought of *as unconsciously undesirable.*

Write your empowering definition of failure here:

_____

_____

_____

_____

_____

_____

_____

_____

_____

_____

_____

2...

Create a NO-Awareness

Most of us are aware of the number of "yesses" we receive during an average week (the number of sales we make, or the number of people we've added to our team).

But when asked exactly how many "noes" we've received, we find it a difficult question to answer.

How about you?

Fill in the blank below:

I am currently getting _____ noes per week.

If you find yourself unable to answer this question, make it a point to count the number of times you hear the word NO. This number will serve as your baseline going forward.

3...

Calculate the Value of Each "NO"

So, what is the value of every NO you receive? Have you ever taken the time to calculate it? Well, here's your chance.

Use the basic math formula below to determine the value of each NO you receive:

Sales $ generated ($_____)

divided by total number of noes received (_____)

=

Dollar Value Per "NO" ($_____)

4...

Change Your Reaction to Hearing NO

On a scale of 1-10, what is your general reaction to hearing NO?

(Circle a number below)

1	2	3	4	5	6	7	8	9	10

Negative   Neutral   Positive

If you're on the negative end of the scale, you have work to do. If you're too far on the positive end of the scale, you have work to do, too. The ideal place to be is in the Neutral Zone.

Next:

When you hear the word "NO", what are the thoughts that run through your mind?

_____

_____

_____

_____

What do these thoughts say to you about your attitudes regarding failure and rejection? Your current level of self-esteem? Resilience? Your belief in your eventual success?

_____

_____

_____

_____

5...

Your Current Persistence Level

Question: How many times are you currently willing to go back to someone who has told you "NO" in the past?

Answer honestly by circling your answer below:

I usually quit after...

Hearing "NO" only one time.

Hearing "NO" a 2nd time.

Hearing "NO" a 3rd time.

Hearing "NO" a 4th time.

Hearing "NO" a 5th time.

More than five times.

6...

Setting "NO-Goals"

My NO-Goal for the next 30-days is to hear "NO"

_____ times

This means hearing _____ noes a day, starting on:

_____/_____/_____.

And I commit to achieving this goal—
no matter how many yeses I get!

7...

Going After Bigger NOs (The Big Fish Exercise)

After hearing more noes, now it's time to work on increasing the size/value of the NO's you're obtaining.

Take a moment to list <u>ten</u> *'Big Fish'* you are committing to approach, even if all you get is "NO"...

1 _____

2 _____

3 _____

4 _____

5 _____

6 _____

7 _____

8 _____

9 _____

10 _____

Now, if you're like most people, you thought of a few people as you did the exercise above, but didn't list them because you thought, *"Why should I bother? They'll just say NO."*

STOP MAKING DECISIONS FOR OTHER PEOPLE! If they want to say NO, let them say no for themselves. So, take another minute and list them here:

1 _____

2 _____

3 _____

4 _____

5 _____

8...

Making an Inventory of Your Previous NO Pipeline

Now, identify people you've approached in the past who said NO to you, and you've treated them as if they meant forever. No doesn't mean never. No means not yet. List them here:

1 _____
2 _____
3 _____
4 _____
5 _____
6 _____
7 _____
8 _____
9 _____
10 _____
11 _____
12 _____
13 _____
14 _____
15 _____
16 _____
17 _____
18 _____
19 _____
20 _____

9...

Identifying Your Limiting Numbers

We all have mental limits and beliefs about various numbers. Take a minute to answer the questions below in regards to your current state of mind and thinking:

What do you currently think is a lot for someone to invest when they join your company?

$_____

Which do you find yourself suggesting first?

_____ The Lowest $ Product/Packages?

_____ The Highest $ Products/Packages?

What do you consider a lot of sales volume for one month?

$_____

What would you consider to be a huge number of people to add to your team in one month?

What other examples of limiting numbers are you currently operating with?

_____

_____

_____

_____

_____

_____

10...

Creating a Vision of Who You Want to Become

Everyone tends to ask:

"How much do I want to make this year?"

Rather than how much did I make, why not ask:

Who do I want to become this year?

Take a moment to write a vision of who you want to become over the next 365 days by learning to Go for No...

_____

_____

_____

_____

_____

_____

_____

_____

_____

_____

_____

_____

_____

_____

_____

Additional Thoughts & Learnings:

_____

_____

_____

_____

_____

_____

_____

_____

_____

_____

_____

_____

_____

_____

_____

_____

_____

_____

_____

_____

_____

_____

_____

_____

_____

_____

_____

_____

THE MILLION

NO

CHALLENGE!

Here is how to participate:

Go to our website at www.goforno.com and click on the

Million NO Challenge

button to discover all the details.

*It's fun
and it's free!*

Are you up for a challenge?

We hope so!

www.goforno.com